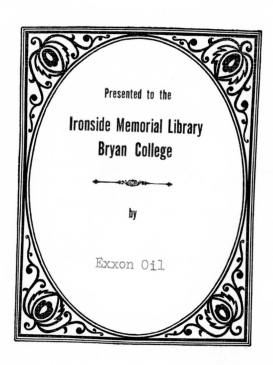

☆

AMERICAN JOURNEYS

☆

Grateful acknowledgment is made to copyright holders listed on pages 190-192, which are hereby made a part of this copyright page.

AMERICAN JOURNEYS

An Anthology of Travel In the United States

Edited by E. D. Bennett

Foreword by Bern Keating

Consulting Editors

Robert N. McCready
John I. White

TravelVision®

A Division of General Drafting Co., Inc.
Convent Station, New Jersey

CONTENTS

FOREWORD
by Bern Keating

The birth pains of the United States began appropriately with a journey—Paul Revere's crucial ride on a borrowed horse across the Massachusetts countryside. In starting a war against the motherland by traveling, Revere exemplified what has become the American genius: the itching foot, the willingness to take to the road for  whatever reason, be it freedom, exploration, riches or a restless spirit.

Even the nomadic tribes of the earth, Bedouins, Gypsies and others, cannot challenge the American people's championship as wanderers. An unremarkable American bourgeois, the kind of man who in Paris or Rome would die in the same bed where he was born and never venture many kilometers from it, was first to make that most stunning of all voyages—to the moon. And only other restless American travelers have followed him.

Our tradition of mobility began with the Indians. The first account in this book tells of the meeting between newly-arrived Pilgrims and the Indian Samoset, who spoke a little English. Though this brief extract does not tell it, from elsewhere we know that Samoset and his friend Squanto, who later moved in with the Pilgrims and guided them through their lean years, had visited England and Newfoundland, and possibly even Spain. Samoset was not even a native of the area, but in good American fashion a visitor from a home farther north. Thus, the

7

meeting between the much-traveled Samoset and the Yorkshiremen who had come to the New World by way of a detour through Holland set the pattern for American life, for neither Indian nor Englishman was on his home ground.

When the coastal strip became crowded with immigrant settlers and the restless young looked inland for new fields, they found that Indians had tramped down a network of forest trails, some of them stamped inches below the surrounding forest floor by generations of moccasined travelers.

Even more important, they found that the Indian had invented a superb water craft, the birchbark canoe. Paddling that most useful explorer's tool, white travelers fanned out into  the interior, riding the network of streams and lakes to the headwaters and carrying the light craft across portages to the headwaters of other streams.

That river network made possible the rapid exploration of the virtually impenetrable forest that closed off the seaboard from the interior, a forest so dense that a squirrel supposedly could have traveled from Charleston to Natchez and never have put his foot to ground. Had not the coastal Americans had the canoe and the more elaborate river craft that followed, the American interior would, like the Congo, have  defied penetration for generations.

The account printed here of the first steamboat trip down the Mississippi tells of the boat's rounding to below Natchez and steaming upriver *against the current*, an event that boggled the sceptical spectators on the riverbank. That mastery of the rushing current opened the vast central basin of the continent to hordes of seacoast dwellers and land-hungry immigrants who swarmed over the land and conquered a wilderness in a single generation.

The acid account of Charles Dickens tells us that, at least as far as riverbank scenery is concerned, little has changed in river travel since his day almost a century and a half ago. In many places even today the river "banks are for the most part

8

deep solitudes, overgrown with trees ... For miles, and miles, and miles these solitudes are unbroken by any sign of human life..." And yet the restless American buys ever more elaborate cruisers and houseboats to explore those rivers, books space on the river steamer, dreams of Huck Finn raft floats down the continent's vast water network.

When the westward-drifting American rambler reached the Plains, the great flat and arid heartland, however, the story changes. Tribal memories of waterways explorations prompted the Plains traveler to call his wagon a Prairie Schooner, but a far cry it was from some of the floating palaces of the great rivers. Dust, thirst, hostile Indians replaced steamboat-boiler explosions as deterrents to the timid—but those desert hazards worked no better than had the massacre of the innocents on exploding steamboats to discourage voyagers.

Restless Americans poured into and across the Plains, bringing with them even their tender young brides, like the charmingly infatuated Susan Magoffin who wrote the diary extract on travel across the prairies.

Mark Twain's account of his stagecoach trip across the prairies shows that even a formidable economic barrier did not stop the flow—for his ticket on the rude and dangerous diligence from Missouri to Nevada cost more than an air ticket over the same route today, and he was allowed only about half the luggage. Nevertheless, stage companies prospered as Americans sought ever more distant horizons.

Pushed back by those dauntless travelers, the frontier receded rapidly. The tart-tongued English lady Isabella Bird is the first of the writers here who tells of a voyage *eastward* from the settled Pacific coast, back toward the interior mountains and plains long since settled and tamed. Cowboy accounts of trail drives of Texas cattle to build northern herds tell of increasing clashes with homesteaders who cut the open range into jealously-guarded plots planted to corn and wheat. Beth O'Shea closes the age of adventurous frontier travel with a cross-country trip in a Model T Ford, a mildly daring adventure, perhaps, for a pair of proper Boston maidens, but no match for the Lewis and Clark journey across the unknown land to the Pacific Northwest.

Were there no frontiers left? The restless American looked skyward.

The world got its first chance to visually witness space exploration when John Glenn made the historic three-orbit voyage he recounts here. And it is no accident that the first man on the moon was an American. As our frontiers have changed, so have our reasons for reaching them. Yet the recent international adventure in space, the rendezvous of American and Soviet astronauts, recalls an earlier meeting—that of Samoset and the Pilgrims.

Surely, the timid might think, the restless American has finally reached the last frontier.

Indeed not, as Arthur C. Clarke's superbly-reasoned and thrilling essay argues. The trip of a band of restless Americans to the moon was just the beginning. Future man will spread throughout the solar system in voyages more stupendous than modern man's imagination can handle. And spearheading that fleet of space travelers probing ever deeper into unthinkably mysterious frontiers will almost certainly be that ultimate nomad, the restless American traveler.

Mr. Keating is a professional travel writer and the author of several books, including The Grand Banks, Alaska!, The Northwest Passage, The Mighty Mississippi, The Gulf Coast and Inside Passage to Alaska. He also contributes regularly to National Geographic and Vista/U.S.A.

THE PILGRIMS MEET A FRIEND

There is a factual record of one of the great journeys of the American experience: The coming of the Pilgrims to New England and the settlement of Plymouth Plantation. A day-by-day journal, written by men who took part in the adventure, was first published in England in 1622. The excerpt which follows describes the encounter in March, 1621, with Samoset, the Indian whose friendly help was invaluable to the colonists in later years. At this first meeting, Samoset seems more at ease and less suspicious than the Pilgrims.

Friday, the 16th, a fair warm day towards; this morning we determined to conclude of the military orders, which we had begun to consider of before but were interrupted by the savages, as we mentioned formerly. And whilst we were busied hereabout, we were interrupted again, for there presented himself a savage, which caused an alarm. He very boldy came all alone and along the houses straight to the rendezvous, where we intercepted him, not suffering him to go in, as undoubtedly he would, out of his boldness. He saluted us in English, and bade us welcome, for he had learned some broken English among the Englishmen that came to fish at Monchiggon [presumably Monhegan Island], and knew by name the most of the captains, commanders, and masters that usually come. He was a man free in speech, so far as he could express his mind, and of a seemly carriage. We questioned him of many things; he

11

was the first savage we could meet withal. He said he was not of these parts, but of Morattiggon [Monhegan Island], and one of the sagamores or lords thereof, and had been eight months in these parts, it lying hence a day's sail with a great wind, and five days by land. He discoursed of the whole country, and of every province, and of their sagamores, and their number of men, and strength. The wind beginning to rise a little, we cast a horseman's coat about him, for he was stark naked, only a leather about his waist with a fringe about a span [nine inches] long, or little more; he had a bow and two arrows, the one headed, and the other unheaded. He was a tall straight man, the hair of his head black, long behind, only short before, none on his face at all; he asked some beer, but we gave him strong water [liquor] and biscuit, and butter, and cheese, and pudding, and a piece of mallard, all which he liked well, and had been acquainted with such amongst the English. He told us the place where we now live is called Patuxet, and that about four years ago all the inhabitants died of an extraordinary plague, and there is neither man, woman, nor child remaining, as indeed we have found none, so as there is none to hinder our possession, or to lay claim unto it. All the afternoon we spent in communication with him; we would gladly have been rid of him at night, but he was not willing to go this night. Then we thought to carry him on shipboard, wherewith he was well content, and went into the shallop, but the wind was high and the water scant, that it could not return back. We lodged him that night at Stephen Hopkin's house, and watched him.

JOURNEYINGS OF THE EASTERN INDIANS

How the aboriginal inhabitants of eastern North America over-
came many of the obstacles to travel presented by the primeval
forests extending from the Atlantic coast to the Mississippi River is
described in the following commentary by historian Seymour Dun-
bar, a direct descendant of Mayflower *passengers John Alden and*
his wife Priscilla Mullins. Condensed from Chapter 2 of his four-
volume work A HISTORY OF TRAVEL IN AMERICA, *published in 1915, this*
begins by quoting a 1694 document giving the reaction of early
white settlers to the same problems as those faced by the red men.

O ne of the best records of the difficulties and
methods of American travel in the early days is contained in a
few words of a lately discovered document written in 1694. In
that year Benjamin Fletcher, Governor of His Majesty's Province
of New York, was planning an attack on the French in Canada,
and he called on his subordinates for a report which should
show the strength of the enemy and by what route and method
of travel he could most easily reach them.

The answer to Governor Fletcher's demand . . . was written by

William Pinhorne and N. Bayard at New York, on July 25 of the year named, and in it they said:

> It is Impossible to march with any party of men to Canada by Land, either in winter or summer, but they must passe a Considerable Part of ye way over ye Lake [Champlain], ye Land on each side being extream steep and Rocky, mountains or els a meer morasse cumbred with underwood, where men cannot goe upright, but must creep throu Bushes for whole days' marches, and impossible for horses to goe at any time of ye year.

The report to Governor Fletcher condenses into a few words certain conditions which dominated all travel in America from the time of its first permanent English occupation until shortly before the Revolution. Those conditions were the use of water routes wherever possible; the uselessness of horses except near settlements or on beaten paths; the necessity of performing extended journeys on foot; and the extreme difficulty of progress through the woods. From the Atlantic Ocean to the Mississippi River—excepting some open country in the region now in part occupied by Indiana, Kentucky and Illinois—the land was covered by a continuous and almost unbroken forest. This wilderness was a thousand miles in extent from east to west, and about as long from north to south. Through it, in every direction, ran countless rivers and their tributaries.

The bulk of the wilderness, as it was until about 1790, was composed of trees that were from two to five feet in diameter. In those regions where the trees grew close together the girth gave way to height, and many reached a hundred and fifty feet into the air. Not until a tree was some six or eight feet in diameter was it considered a large one and those that attracted the attention of travellers, and were measured, were ten, twelve and sometimes even fifteen feet in thickness.

The earth beneath these huge growths was cumbered with fallen trees of all sizes and in all stages of decay. The hurricanes that now do occasional damage to towns and farms regularly wrought their havoc in the wilderness, and the confusion and tangle of the forest after the visit of such a storm can easily be pictured. Up from the earth made rich by ages of decayed vegetation sprang all manner of thickets and similar small growths that sometimes choked the lower spaces and were

14

frequently bound together by a snarl of vines tough as wires or as big as a man's wrist. The rains or melting snows left such soil very slowly, and that is why there are frequent references, in olden records, to swamps or morasses which then occupied sections that have long since become dry and solid ground.

The human habitants of this vast and gloomy region, in which the sun's rays in places never reached the ground, were two or three hundred thousand copper-colored natives, whose numbers were too small to have made any impression on it, even had they been so inclined. But they were not so purposed. Instead, they were peculiarly in harmony and sympathy with their home, and desired that it should remain always as they knew it. The few agricultural clearings made by some of the Indians who lived north of the Ohio River, by the Iroquois in what is now central New York state, and elsewhere, were trivial gashes amid the universal woods. When the Indians travelled they moved by water if their purpose made it possible. For their land travel they created paths leading from one stream to another. In going across country they had a wonderful faculty for establishing routes that were, in an economic sense, the best that could be chosen. An Indian overland trail always led the traveller to his destination in less time, or with fewer physical obstacles to overcome, than any other course that could be selected between the two points which it connected.

These Indian trails—the corner-stone of land travel in America—were from twelve to eighteen inches in width, and sometimes, when they led through regions where the native travel was particularly heavy and long continued, were worn a foot deep by generations of soft moccasins.

The forest roads of the natives—first aids to such land travel as was attempted in early days by the white population of America—were not the only contribution made by the red men to the methods of the newcomers. From them, also, was taken the earliest form of water craft. The canoe, as used by the Indians and at once adopted by the whites, was of two very different forms. One was made from a log of suitable size, and the other from the bark of trees, especially the birch, spruce, or elm. The use of these two types, both by the Indians and afterward by white invaders, depended on the nature of the waters to be navigated, the desire for speed, and the frequent

15

necessity of making portages from one stream to another. To some extent also the type was a geographical one, since the birch tree from the bark of which the best kind of bark canoe was made was not so plentiful in the South as in the North. For a heavy wooden canoe a fallen log was selected that, while still entirely sound, had become somewhat seasoned. Sometimes a standing tree was chosen by the Indians and felled by means of hatchets or fire. A section of the trunk from fifteen to thirty feet long and about three feet in diameter was then cut out and elevated from the ground, for convenience in carrying on the work. The log was shaped and hollowed by fire and cutting implements, and a very strong and serviceable, though rough and slow moving craft was obtained.

In fashioning the much more graceful, mobile and useful birch-bark canoe the Indian selected his tree, made a straight vertical incision in the bark from near the base of the trunk to a spot at the height of his head, and then, with utmost care, peeled the bark from the tree by the aid of his knife. The framework of the craft was made of thin strips of cedar or spruce, and the birch-bark covering was attached to it by long, tough, slender, fibrous roots of the larch or balsam, which had previously been manipulated into extreme pliability. The various strips of birch-bark were also sewed together with the same sort of roots, and, before being fastened to the framework, were cut to the necessary pattern. The boat was then completed and given its final shape by the insertion of the many narrow and elastic ribs of spruce. All seams and cracks were covered with hot pitch from the balsam or spruce, and the canoe was water-tight and ready for use. Each tribe had its own pattern or style for its canoes, and they varied in size from ten or twelve feet to fifty or sixty feet in length.

In this wonderful and famous boat, created by the woodcraft genius of the Indian from the materials immediately about him, he could travel for thousands of miles if need be. When he came to the head waters of a stream, where the current no longer afforded the few inches of depth necessary to carry him on his way, he could pick up his canoe and carry it for miles to another lake or river. In times of storm it served him as a snug shelter, and the forest was a factory where it could be repaired, or even replaced, at any time, with prompt delivery guaranteed.

DOBBIN IN COLONIAL AMERICA

Almost everyone knows that the early Spaniards who explored the New World brought horses with them. Less well known is the fact that the English colonists who settled the eastern seaboard began importing and breeding horses almost immediately. Although the first equine arrivals at Jamestown, in 1610, became food for starving Virginians, others that landed in 1611 and shortly thereafter fared better and served their usual purpose. The Mayflower *on its historic 1620 voyage carried no animals larger than goats and, rather oddly, the Plymouth Pilgrims were still depending on "shank's mare" for transport when the first Puritans arrived at Salem, in 1628, with a small herd of horses aboard their cramped vessels. The next year an enterprising Pilgrim put in an order for a shipment from England, which soon enabled the men of Plymouth to take to the saddle. Settlers in the Carolinas and Georgia, in addition to bringing stock across the Atlantic, were able to obtain from the Indians a breed of horse, slightly smaller than English types, known as the Chickasaw, originally brought to Florida from Spain. The Dutchmen who raised their flag over New Amsterdam imported heavy draft animals.*

With most of the eastern region covered by nearly impenetrable forest, horses in early colonial days were used largely for plowing and riding over narrow woods trails. For a hundred years or so roads were almost non-existent and wheeled vehicles extremely scarce. The invention during the first half of the eighteenth century of the famous six-horse Conestoga freight wagon, a product of the "Pennsylvania Dutch" country west of Philadelphia, brought a great change. How this and other horse-drawn conveyances gradually revolutionized transportation is told by Robert West Howard in an excerpt from his 1965 volume THE HORSE IN AMERICA.

Even in progressive Pennsylvania, road construction lagged for decades after the introduction of the Conestogans' wagon-hitch. This was due, as Stevenson W. Fletcher diagnosed it, to "the policy of placing responsibility for building and maintaining roads solely on local governments.... Few streams were bridged; fords were difficult and often dangerous; ferries, which were privately owned, were few and crude. Rails were piled by the roadside for use in prying wagons out of the mud.... A teamster who was stalled in the mud might have to wade in and unhitch his team and spend the night by the side of the road until assistance came."

The other colonies were even more isolated or, to coin a phrase, trail-confined. The best transportation was by boat. But all of the rivers ran west-to-east off the mountain ranges. This limited most inter-colony travel to an ocean voyage, a horseback journey, or walking. All were perilous.

The trappers, hunters, Indian traders and frontiersmen used trains of shaggy horses, usually only thirteen hands high [a hand is 4 inches] and hitched in tandem, to pack their goods in and out of the wilderness. A horse could carry one hundred and eighty to two hundred pounds on its pack saddle. Freight rates were exorbitant. In 1784 the pack-horse fee for delivering a ton of trade goods or household equipment from eastern Pennsylvania to the new village of Erie on Lake Erie was $249.

Planters, preachers and government officials rode over the pack-pony trails on Narragansetts, Chickasaws or Galloways. Most of their horses were between fourteen and fifteen hands high and weighed about one thousand pounds. Luggage was limited to the few items that could be forced into their saddlebags alongside food supplies and a reserve supply of lead, wadding and gunpowder for the musket or pistol. A horseback journey between New York and Boston in 1750 took twelve days, an average of seventeen miles a day. Travelers were such a rarity in some areas that the courts ordered innkeepers to notify the local constable whenever a person applied for lodging.

Except for the red-white-and-blue Conestogas on Philadelphia-Susquehanna Valley lanes, wagons were a rarity. During the spring of 1755, General Braddock sent agents into Virginia and Maryland to lease wagons for the baggage train of the expedition against Forts Duquesne and Niagara. They rode back to the army's camp on the Potomac with the news that only twenty-five wagons fit for the wilderness journey existed in all of Virginia and Maryland. In desperation, Braddock appealed to Benjamin Franklin, newly appointed Postmaster General for the Northern Colonies. Franklin hurriedly printed handbills, in which he personally guaranteed that "fair wages" would be paid, and sent them via Post Riders to be displayed at every church, store and blacksmith shop in the Conestoga country. Within two weeks, Braddock had 155 fully equipped Conestoga wagons at the camp.

A survey taken in 1761 indicated that only eighteen families in Pennsylvania owned carriages. The sedan chair, carried on poles by four footmen (i.e. runners), was the only conveyance vaguely resembling a public transportation vehicle, and not more than twenty-five of them existed in the thirteen colonies.

Already famous as editor of the *Pennsylvania Gazette* and as the puckish author of *Poor Richard's Almanac*, Ben Franklin in 1754 received King George II's appointment as Postmaster General for the North. At the time he secured the wagons for the Braddock expedition, he was reorganizing the haphazard system for inter-colony mail deliveries. He recruited a corps of young horsemen to serve as Post Riders, and announced that it would maintain year-round deliveries between Philadelphia and Boston. The schedule, he promised, would average forty miles a day, requiring a week for the ride from the west bank of the Delaware to the south bank of the Charles.

Next, Franklin began a campaign to improve the inter-colony trails. The threat of French and Indian invasions in Pennsylvania, New Jersey, New York and New England during 1755-56 and the difficulties experienced in delivering supplies to the New York and St. Lawrence Valley campaigns against the

French during 1756-59 sustained his arguments. Soon after word reached Philadelphia that the Treaty of Paris had been signed on February 10, 1763, and the French and Indian Wars were over, Franklin decided on a maneuver that would publicize the "better roads" campaign and—since postal fees were based on a mileage rate—to simplify the Post Riders' bookkeeping.

During the summer of 1763, Franklin and his daughter, Sally, drove a gig, or perhaps a one-horse chaise, from New York City to Boston. The vehicle is reputed to have been equipped with a hardwood slat attached to one of the wheel-rims. Each time the wheel turned, the slat clacked against an iron peg projecting from the carriage body. Franklin had measured the circumference of the wheel and figured out the number of clacks per mile. He drove the horse. Sally counted the clacks, then shrilled "Ho!" at the end of each mile. At this signal Franklin stopped the horse, climbed down, and pulled a stake from the bundle beneath the seat. He scratched Roman numerals and capital letters on the stake, jammed it into the dirt at the roadside, and drove on.

Miles behind the carriage, a cart loaded with engraved slabs of stone creaked along the trail. When the cart reached one of the stakes, the teamster and his helper unloaded the proper slab, carried it over to the stake and dug a hole. Tamped upright in the hole, with its semispherical top eighteen inches above the ground, the stone displayed the same numerals and letters that Franklin had scratched on the stake. A typical one told travelers:

N.H.
XVI
M

It indicated that the stone stood "to the clack" sixteen miles from New Haven.

With the final stone set up, probably on Boston Common, America had its first set of highway markers. Franklin's installation of the labeled stone posts, plus his organization of the Post Riders, gave the New York-Boston throughway the name it still bears: the Boston Post Road.

All along the way Franklin also harangued New York, Connecticut, Rhode Island and Massachusetts officials into agreement on a system of highway improvements and maintenance. Some towns began to permit farmers to work off annual taxes by removing stumps and cobbles from the right-of-way, or laying corduroys of logs across boggy sections, or building bridges over creeks. Other communities organized convicts and "public offenders" into chain-gangs for work on road construction. Although the result was a hazardous strip of quagmire, hub-deep ruts, and steep hills, it enabled the use of carriages, freight wagons and the first "publick conveyances" between New England and New York City.

The first American coaches were springless box wagons. When they traveled over level countryside, the passengers could ride on wooden cross planks doweled between the sideboards of the box. But on uphill pulls, or across bogs, everybody walked—and often helped to push the coach.

Our first scheduled coach service seems to have been a weekly trip started by the Moravians of Bethlehem, Pennsylvania, in 1742 to deliver mail and travelers to and from Philadelphia. In 1756, a John Butler established a line between Philadelphia and New York that took three days for the hundred-mile journey and included six ferryboat rides. An "express coach" service between Philadelphia and New York began biweekly service during the 1760s. It used four-horse teams, maintained a schedule of forty-eight hours through most of the year, and called its vehicles "The Flying Machines."

During the 1760s, too, initial efforts were made to surface the principal streets and market places of cities with cobblestone or brick paving. Benjamin Franklin preferred plank highways and promoted them; a few short stretches were laid along waterfronts and in the vicinity of iron furnaces and shipyards. These experiments, all manifestations of an oncoming horse-and-wagon age, influenced the blacksmith and wainwright professions.

Before 1750, few American horses were shod. Few blacksmiths knew how to trim hooves, hammer out the proper size and shape of horseshoes and fit them. But the new cobblestone and brick paving, plank roads and "corduroys" caused the same wear and splintering on the hooves of colonial drafters and saddlers that the stone "Vias" had inflicted on the Romans' mail-carrier mounts. So the regime of the blacksmith shop as the town center for horsemen developed during the decade preceding the Revolution.

Post roads and paving on city streets naturally encouraged the sale of horse-drawn vehicles. Scores of wainwright shops opened. These usually began as a sideline production at the blacksmith shops, then, as the Wagon Age clattered in, grew into separate industries that employed wheelwrights, turners, whitesmiths, harnessmakers, and similar parts specialists.

The Wagon Age shaped quickly after Yorktown. On April 16, 1789, General George Washington left Mount Vernon in a white coach that was to carry him 250 miles to the presidential inauguration ceremony in New York City. The coach was a radical new vehicle. Its body was egg-shaped and had glass windows leaded into the doors on each side. Padded leather cushions and back-rests were suspended across the interior. This "cab" hung three feet above the ground on a leather cradle anchored on the axles of the tall rear wheels and small front wheels. The driver and footman rode outside on a padded seat built five feet above the front wheels. A four-horse team of matched gray trotters, each about fifteen hands high, was hitched to the single drawing-pole. At a dozen "refreshment and speech-making" stops along the route, relay teams of gray horses awaited their proud hours in the journey.

Washington's seven-day trip was a triumph for the new Wagon Age as well as for the new United States of America. Hundreds of planters, merchants and army officers drove gigs, chariots, shays and buggies down to the Post Roads, so that their families could join in the waving and bowing as Washington's coach cantered by.

BEN FRANKLIN ARRIVES AT PHILADELPHIA

Following a falling-out with his brother-employer James, publisher of a newspaper, seventeen-year-old Benjamin Franklin left his native city of Boston and took passage on a sloop for New York to seek employment there as a printer. In this he was unsuccessful, but he was told that he probably could find work in Philadelphia. Accordingly, leaving his belòngings to be sent by sea, he set out from New York on a fifty-mile hike to the New Jersey town of Burlington on the Delaware River, where he hoped to find a boat that would take him to his destination. In his autobiography, Franklin describes his adventures along the way and his first day in the city that was to be so closely associated with him throughout his long and illustrious career as a printer, publisher, author and statesman. The year was 1723.

It rained very hard all the day; I was thoroughly soak'd, and by noon a good deal tired; so I stopt at a poor inn, where I staid all night, beginning now to wish that I had never left home. I cut so miserable a figure, too, that I found, by the questions ask'd me, I was suspected to be some run-away servant, and in danger of being taken up on that suspicion. However, I proceeded the next day, and got in the evening to an inn, within eight or ten miles of Burlington, kept by one Dr. Brown. He entered into conversation with me while I took some refreshment, and, finding I had read a little, became very sociable and friendly. Our acquaintance continu'd as long as he liv'd. He had been, I imagine, an itinerant doctor, for there was no town in England, or country in Europe, of which he could not give a very particular account. He had some letters, and was ingenious, but much of an unbeliever, and wickedly undertook, some years after, to travestie the Bible in doggrel verse, as [Charles] Cotton had done Virgil. By this means he set many of the facts in a very ridiculous light, and might have hurt weak minds if his work had been published; but it never was.

At his house I lay that night, and the next morning reach'd Burlington, but had the mortification to find that the regular boats were gone a little before my coming, and no other expected to go before Tuesday, this being Saturday; wherefore I returned to an old woman in the town, of whom I had bought gingerbread to eat on the water, and ask'd her advice. She invited me to lodge at her house till a passage by water should offer; and being tired with my foot travelling, I accepted the invitation. She understanding I was a printer, would have had me stay at that town and follow my business, being ignorant of the stock necessary to begin with. She was very hospitable, gave me a dinner of ox-cheek with great good will, accepting only of a pot of ale in return; and I thought myself fixed till Tuesday should come. However, walking in the evening by the side of the river, a boat came by, which I found was going towards Philadelphia, with several people in her. They took me in, and, as there was no wind, we row'd all the way; and about midnight, not having yet seen the city, some of the company were confident we must have passed it, and would row no farther; the others knew not where we were; so we put toward the shore, got into a creek, landed near an old fence, with the rails of which we made a fire, the night being cold, in October, and there we remained till daylight. Then one of the company knew the place to be Cooper's Creek, a little above Philadelphia, which we saw as soon as we got out of the creek, and arriv'd there about eight or nine o'clock on the Sunday morning, and landed at the Market-street wharf.

I have been the more particular in this description of my journey, and shall be so of my first entry into that city, that you may in your mind compare such unlikely beginnings with the figure I have since made there. I was in my working dress, my best clothes being to come round by sea. I was dirty from my journey; my pockets were stuff'd out with shirts and stockings, and I knew no soul nor where to look for lodging. I was fatigued with travelling, rowing, and want of rest, I was very hungry; and my whole stock of cash consisted of a Dutch dollar, and about a shilling in copper. The latter I gave the people of the boat for my passage, who at first refus'd it, on account of my rowing; but I insisted on their taking it. A man being sometimes more generous when he has but a little money than when he has plenty, perhaps thro' fear of being thought to have but little.

Then I walked up the street, gazing about till near the market-house I met a boy with bread. I had made many a meal on bread, and, inquiring where he got it, I went immediately to the baker's he directed me to, in Second-street, and ask'd for bisket, intending such as we had in Boston; but they, it seems, were not made in Philadelphia. Then I asked for a three-penny loaf, and was told they had none such. So not considering or knowing the difference of money, and the greater cheapness nor the names of his bread, I bad him give me three-penny worth of any sort. He gave me, accordingly, three great puffy rolls. I was surpriz'd at the quantity, but took it, and, having no room in my pockets, walk'd off with a roll under each arm, and eating the other. Thus I went up Market-street as far as Fourth-street, passing by the door of Mr. Read, my future wife's father; when she, standing at the door, saw me, and thought I made, as I certainly did, a most awkward, ridiculous appearance. Then I turned and went down Chestnut-street and part of Walnut-street, eating my roll all the way, and, coming round, found myself again at Market-street wharf, near the boat I came in, to which I went for a draught of the river water; and, being filled with one of my rolls, gave the other two to a woman and her child that came down to the river in the boat with us, and were waiting to go farther.

Thus refreshed, I walked again up the street, which by this time had many clean-dressed people in it, who were all walking the same way. I joined them, and thereby was led into the great meeting-house of the Quakers near the market. I sat down among them, and, after looking round awhile and hearing nothing said, being very drowsy thro' labor and want of rest the preceding night, I fell fast asleep, and continued so till the meeting broke up, when one was kind enough to rouse me. This was, therefore, the first house I was in or slept in, in Philadelphia.

A 1750 VIEW OF NIAGARA

One of the best early descriptions of the wonders of Niagara Falls written in English is the following by a Swedish naturalist, Peter Kalm. It is excerpted from a letter penned by Kalm to noted Philadelphia botanist John Bartram and is date-lined "Albany, September 2, 1750." Kalm's letter appeared in Bartram's book OBSERVATIONS, *published in London the following year.*

As Kalm's journey took place prior to the French and Indian War, Fort Niagara on Lake Ontario at the mouth of the Niagara River, and the surrounding region, were still under French control. The "Father Hennepin" who is belittled in Kalm's letter was Louis Hennepin, the Belgian friar who came to Canada in 1675 and accompanied LaSalle on his explorations. Hennepin wrote several interesting books about his travels, but some of his claims were later discredited. As the dimensions which Kalm gives for the falls vary considerably from those in any modern encyclopedia, he, too, appears to have estimated none too well, or perhaps to have been the victim of typographical errors. All of his observations were made from what is now the New York side of the river.

It is of interest to note that in the more than 200 years since Kalm's letter was written, the appearance of the falls on the Canadian side has altered drastically. Erosion has pushed their center upstream nearly a quarter of a mile.

After a fatiguing travel, first on horseback thro' the country of the Six Indian Nations, to Oswego, and from thence in a canoe upon lake Ontario, I came on the 12th of August in the evening to Niagara fort. The French there seemed much perplexed at my coming, imagining I was an English officer, who, under pretext of seeing Niagara Falls, came with some other view. But as soon as I shewed them my passports they changed their behaviour and received me with great civility. Niagara Fall is six French leagues from Niagara fort. You first go three leagues by water up Niagara river, and then three leagues over the carrying-place. As it was late when I arrived at the Fort, I could not the same day go to the Fall, but I prepared myself to do it the next morning. At break of day I set out.

The commandant, Monsr. Beaujon, had given orders to two of the officers of the Fort to go with me and shew me everything, and also sent by them an order to Monsr. Jonqueire, who had liv'd ten years by the carrying-place, and knew everything worth notice of the Fall, better than any other person, to go with me, and shew and tell me whatever he knew. A little before we came to the carrying-place, the water of the Niagara River grew so rapid that four men in a light birch canoe had much difficulty to get up thither. Canoes can go half a league above the beginning of the carrying-place, tho' they must work against a water extremely rapid; but higher up it is quite impossible, the whole course of the water for two leagues and a half up to the great Fall being a series of smaller Falls, one under another, in which the greatest canoe or battoe would in a moment be turned upside down. We went ashore, therefore, and walked over the carrying-place, having besides the high and steep side of the river, two great hills to ascend. Here on the carrying-place I saw above 200 Indians, most of them belonging to the Six Nations, busy in carying packs of furs, chiefly of deer and bear, over the carrying-place. You would be surpriz'd to see what abundance of these things are brought every day over this place. An Indian gets 20 pence for every pack he carries over, the distance being three leagues. Half an hour past 10 in the morning we came to the great Fall, which I found as follows.

The river, or rather strait, runs here from S.S.E. to N.N.W. and the rocks of the great Fall crosses it, not in a right line, but forming almost the figure of a semicircle or horseshoe. Above the Fall, in the middle of the river, is an island, lying also S.S.E. and N.N.W. or parallel with the sides of the river. Its length is about 7 or 8 French arpents. The lower end of this island is just at the perpendicular edge of the Fall.

Before the water comes to this island it runs but slowly, compared with its motion when it approaches the island, where it grows the most rapid water in the World, running with a surprizing swiftness before it comes to the Fall. It is quite white, and in many places is thrown high up into the air! The greatest and strongest battoes would here in a moment be turned over and over. The water that goes down on the west side of the island is more rapid, in greater abundance, whiter, and seems almost to outdo an arrow in swiftness. When you are at the Fall and look up the river, you may see that the river above the Fall is everywhere exceeding steep, almost as the side of a hill. When all this water comes to the very Fall, there it throws itself down perpendicular! It is beyond all belief the surprize when you see this! You cannot see it without being quite terrified; to behold so vast a quantity of water falling headlong from a surprizing height.

I doubt not but you have a desire to learn the exact height of this great Fall. Father Hennepin supposes it 600 feet perpendicular. But he has gained little credit in Canada. The name of honour they give him there is *un grand Menteur*, or The Great Liar; he writes of what he saw in places where he never was. 'Tis true he saw this Fall, but as it is the way of some travellers to magnify everything, so has he done with regard to the fall of Niagara. This humour of travellers has occasioned me many disappointments in my travels, having seldom been so happy as to find the wonderful things that had been related by others. For my part, who am not fond of the Marvellous, I like to see things just as they are and so to relate them. Since Father Hennepin's time this Fall, by all accounts that have been given of it, has grown less and less, and those who have measur'd it with mathmatical instruments find the perpendicular fall of the water to be exactly 137 feet. Mons. Morandrier, the king's engineer in Canada, assured me, and gave it me also under his hand, that 137 feet was precisely the height of it. It is true, those who have tried to measure it with a line find it sometimes 140, sometimes 150 feet, and sometimes more. But the reason is it cannot be measured with any certainty, the water carrying away the line.

From the place where the water falls there rise abundance of vapours, like the greatest and thickest smoak. These vapours rise high in the air when it is calm, but are dispers'd by the wind when it blows hard. If you go nigh to this vapour or fog, or if the wind blows it on you, it is so penetrating that in a few minutes you will be as wet as if you had been under water.

Several of the French gentlemen told me that when birds come flying into this fog or smoak of the Fall, they fall down and perish in the water, either because their wings are become wet or that the noise of the Fall astonishes them and they know not where to go in the dark. But others were of opinion that seldom or never any bird perishes there in that manner, because, as they all agreed, among the abundance of birds found dead below the Fall there are no other sorts than such as live and swim frequently in the water, as swans, geese, ducks, water-hens, teal and the like. And very often great flocks of them are seen going to destruction in this manner; they swim in the river above the Fall and so are carried down lower and lower by the water, as water-fowl commonly take great delight in being carry'd by the stream, so here they indulge themselves in enjoying this pleasure so long that 'tis no longer possible for them to rise, but they are driven down the precipice to perish. They are observ'd when they draw nigh the Fall to endeavour with all their might to take wing and leave the water, but they cannot. In the months of September and October such abundant quantities of dead water-fowl are found every morning below the Fall, on the shore, that the garrison of the fort for a long time live chiefly upon them. Besides the fowl they find also several sorts of dead fish, also deer, bears, and other animals which have tried to cross the water above the Fall. The larger animals are generally found broken to pieces. Just below the Fall the water is not rapid but goes in circles and whirls like a boiling pot, which however doth not hinder the Indians going upon it in small canoes a fishing.

Every day when the sun shines, you see here from 10 o'clock in the morning to 2 in the afternoon, below the Fall and under you, when you stand at the side over the Fall, a glorious rainbow and sometimes two rainbows, one within the other. I was so happy to be at the Fall on a fine clear day, and it was with great delight I view'd this rainbow, which had almost all the colours you see in a rainbow in the air. The more vapours, the brighter and clearer is the rainbow.

Here you have, Sir, a short but exact description of this famous Niagara cataract. You may depend on the truth of what I write. You must excuse me if you find in my account no extravagant wonders. I cannot make nature otherwise than I find it. I had rather it be said of me in time to come that I related things as they were and that all is found to agree with my description, than to be esteemed a false Relater. I have seen some other things in this my journey, an account of which I know would gratify your curiosity, but time at present will not permit me to write more, and I hope shortly to see you.

DR. HAMILTON'S OBSERVATIONS

A down-to-earth view of life along the northeastern seaboard of America three decades prior to the Revolution fills the travel diary of 32-year-old Dr. Alexander Hamilton, a well-to-do, Scottish-born physician of Annapolis, Maryland. Seeking to improve his health, Dr. Hamilton set out on horseback May 30, 1744 on a leisurely journey that took him to Philadelphia, New York (where he enjoyed a side trip by boat to the Dutch town of Albany), out to the eastern tip of Long Island, by ferry to New London, Connecticut, to Boston, and York, Maine. On returning, he followed the Connecticut shore to New York, thence home via Philadelphia. As would be said today, he didn't miss a trick, or a pretty face, and he put it all down on paper. His manuscript allegedly remained in the possession of an Italian gentleman to whom it was dedicated until somewhere around 1900. An Italian bookseller sent it to London where it was sold and resold until William K. Bixby printed 487 copies for private distribution in 1907.

MARBLEHEAD

At one o'clock I arrived at Marblehead, a large fishing town, lying upon the sea coast, built upon a rock, and standing pretty bleak to the easterly winds from the sea. It lies eighteen miles northeast from Boston, and is somewhat larger than Albany, but not so neatly or compactly built, the houses being all of wood and the streets very uneven, narrow, and irregular. It contains about 5,000 inhabitants and their commodity is fish. There is round the town above 200 acres of land covered with fish-flakes, upon which they dry their cod. There are ninety fishing sloops always employed, and they deal for

30

L 34,000 sterling prime cost value in fish yearly, bringing in 30,000 quintals— a quintal being one hundredweight dried fish, which is 3,000,000 pounds' weight, a great quantity of that commodity.

SALEM

Mr. Malcom and I returned to Salem a little before eight o'clock, and went to the Ship Tavern, where we drank punch and smoaked tobacco with several colonels; for colonels, captains, and majors are so plenty here that they are to be met with in all companies, and yet methinks they look no more like soldiers than they look like divines; but they are gentlemen of the place, and that is sufficient.

The town of Salem is a pretty place, being the first settled place in New England. In it there is one Church of England, one Quaker meeting, and five Presbyterian meetings.

CAMBRIDGE

When we came to Cambridge we waited upon Mr. Hollyhoak, the president, who sent the librarian to show us the college and the library. Cambridge is a scattered town about the largeness of Annapolis, and is delightfully situated upon a pleasant plain near a pretty river of the same name, over which is a wooden bridge. The college is a square building or quadrangle about 150 feet every way. The building upon the left hand as you enter the court is the largest and handsomest and most ancient, being about 100 years old; but the middle or front building is indifferent, and of no taste. That upon the right hand has a little clock upon it, which has a very good bell. In the library are three or four thousand volumes with some curious editions of the classics, presented to the college by Dean Barklay. There are some curiosities, the best of which is the cut of a tree about ten inches thick and eight long, entirely petrified and turned into stone.

DEDHAM

I had a solitary ride to Dedham, where I breakfasted at Fisher's and had some comical chat with Betty, the landlady's daughter, a jolly buxom girl. The country people here are full of salutations, even the country girls that are scarce old enough to walk will curtsy to one passing by.

A FROLIC AMONG THE STRAWBERRIES

Beginning in 1773, youthful naturalist William Bartram spent four years journeying through the South, making voluminous notes on the flora, fauna, and other matters. For the general reader, perhaps the most interesting portions of his resulting volume, TRAVELS, *reissued by Yale University Press in 1958, are his engaging descriptions of the Southern Indians of two centuries ago—their social customs, agricultural pursuits, manner of dress, and their amusements. That Bartram was a great admirer of the first Americans is obvious from the following account of a chance encounter that he and a companion, a white trader, had near the present site of the mountain town of Franklin, North Carolina. It reads almost like a passage from Greek mythology.*

We returned to our trusty servants that were regaling themselves in the exuberant sweet pastures and strawberry fields in sight, and mounted again; proceeding on our return to town, continued through part of this high forest skirting on the meadows; began to ascend the hills of a ridge which we were under the necessity of crossing, and having gained its summit, enjoyed a most enchanting view, a vast expanse of green meadows and strawberry fields; a meandering river gliding through, saluting in its various turnings the swelling, green, turfy knolls, embellished with parterres of flowers and fruitful strawberry beds; flocks of turkeys strolling about them; herds of deer prancing in the meads or bounding over the hills; companies of young, innocent Cherokee virgins, some busily gathering the rich fragrant fruit, others having already filled their baskets, lay reclined under the shade of floriferous and fragrant

32

native bowers of Magnolia, Azalea, Philadelphus, perfumed Calycanthus, sweet Yellow Jessamine and cerulian Glycine frutescens, disclosing their beauties to the fluttering breeze, and bathing their limbs in the cool fleeting streams; whilst other parties, more gay and libertine, were yet collecting strawberries or wantonly chasing their companions, tantalising them, staining their lips and cheeks with the rich fruit.

This sylvan scene of primitive innocence was enchanting, and perhaps too enticing for hearty young men long to continue idle spectators.

In fine, nature prevailing over reason, we wished at least to have a more active part in their delicious sports. Thus precipitately resolving, we cautiously made our approaches, yet undiscovered, almost to the joyous scene of action. Now, although we meant no other than an innocent frolic with this gay assembly of hamadryades, we shall leave it to the person of feeling and sensibility to form an idea to what lengths our passions might have hurried us, thus warmed and excited, had it not been for the vigilance and care of some envious matrons who lay in ambush, and espying us gave the alarm, time enough for the nymphs to rally and assemble together; we however pursued and gained ground on a group of them, who had incautiously strolled to a greater distance from their guardians, and finding their retreat now like to be cut off, took shelter under cover of a little grove, but on perceiving themselves to be discovered by us, kept their [station] peeping through the bushes; when observing our approaches, they confidently discovered themselves and decently advanced to meet us, half unveiling their blooming faces, incarnated with the modest maiden blush, and with native innocence and cheerfulness, presented their little baskets, merrily telling us their fruit was ripe and sound.

We accepted a basket, sat down and regaled ourselves on the delicious fruit, encircled by the whole assembly of the innocently jocose sylvan nymphs; by this time the several parties under the conduct of the elder matrons, had disposed themselves in companies on the green, turfy banks.

My young companion, the trader, by concessions and suitable apologies for the bold intrusion, having compromised the matter with them, engaged them to bring their collections to his house at a stipulated price, we parted friendly.

WASHINGTON TOURS THE SOUTH

In 1791, two years after his inauguration as first President, George Washington set out from Philadelphia on a tour of the South which included stops, both going and coming, at Mount Vernon and two visits to Georgetown, Maryland, for checking on the early stages of the new federal capital planned for the banks of the Potomac. As befitted a great national hero, he was everywhere wined and dined, escorted over the dusty roads by mounted militia, honored at balls and receptions. Each night by candlelight he noted the events of the day in his diary. A sampling of these entries follows. The "Majr. Jackson" whom Washington names as his traveling companion was Major William Jackson, a secretarial aide.

Monday, March 21st.
Left Philadelphia about 11 o'clock to make a tour through the Southern States. Reached Chester about 3 o'clock—dined and lodged at Mr. Wythes. Roads exceedingly deep, heavy and cut in places by the Carriages which used them.

In this tour I was accompanied by Majr. Jackson,—my equipage and attendance consisted of a Charriot and four horses drove in hand—a light baggage Waggon and two horses—four saddle horses besides a led one for myself—and five—to wit;—my Valet de Chambre, two footmen, Coachmen and postilion.

Sunday, March 27th.

About 9 o'clock this morning I left Annapollis, under a discharge of Artillery, and being accompanied by the Governor and a Mr. Kilty of the Council and Mr. Charles Stuart proceeded on my journey for George-Town. Bated at Queen Ann, 13 miles distant and lodged at Bladensburgh.

Thursday, April 7th.

In attempting to cross the ferry at Colchester [Virginia] with the four horses hitched to the Chariot by the neglect of the person who stood before them, one of the leaders got overboard when the boat was in swimming water and 50 yards from the shore—with much difficulty he escaped drowning before he could be disengaged. His struggling frightened the others in such a manner that one after another and in quick succession they all got overboard harnessed and fastened as they were and with the utmost difficulty they were saved and the Carriage escaped been dragged after them, as the whole of it happened in swimming water and at a distance from the shore. Providentially—indeed miraculously—by the exertions of people who went off in Boats and jumped into the River as soon as the Batteau was forced into wading water—no damage was sustained by the horses, Carriage or harness.

Tuesday, April 12th.

In company with the Governor [Beverley Randolph], the Directors of the James River Navigation Company, the Manager and many other Gentlemen, I viewed the Canal, Sluces, Locks, and other works between the City of Richmond and Westham.

Thursday, April 14th.

Left Richmond after an early breakfast, and passing through Manchester received a Salute from cannon and an Escort of Horse under the command of Captn. David Meade Randolph as far as Osbornes when I was met by the Petersburgh horse and escorted to that place, and partook of a Public dinner given by the Mayor and Corporation and went to an Assembly in the evening for the occasion at which there were between 60 and 70 ladies.

Monday, April 18th.

Set out by six o'clock—dined at a small house kept by one

Slaughter, 22 Miles from Hallifax and lodged at Tarborough 14 Miles further. Corn, Porke, and some Tar are exports from it.

Thursday, April 21st.
Dined with the Citizens [of New Bern] at a public dinner given by them; and went to a dancing assembly in the evening: both of which was at what they call the Pallace, formerly the Government House and a good brick building but now hastening to Ruins. The Company at both was numerous, at the latter there were abt. 70 ladies.

Monday, May 2nd.
Breakfasted at the Country seat of Govr. Pinckney about 18 miles from our lodging place, and then came to the ferry at Haddrel's point, 6 miles further, where I was met by the Recorder of the City [Charleston], General Pinckney and Edward Rutledge, Esqr. in a 12 oared barge rowed by 12 American Captains of Ships, most elegantly dressed. There were a great number of other Boats with Gentlemen and ladies in them; and two Boats with Music; all of whom attended me across, and on the passage were met by a number of others.

Tuesday, May 3rd.
Breakfasted with Mrs. Rutledge (the Lady of the Chief Justice of the State who was on the Circuits) and dined with the Citizens at a public dinr. given by them at the Exchange.
Was visited about 2 O'clock by a great number of the most respectable ladies of Charleston—the first honor of the kind I had ever experienced and it was as flattering as it was singular.

Thursday, May 12th.
By five o'clock we set out from Judge Hayward's and road to Purisburgh 22 miles to breakfast.
At that place I was met by Messrs. Jones, Colo. Habersham, Mr. Jno. Houston, Genl. McIntosh and Mr. Clay, a Comee. from the City of Savanna to conduct me thither. Boats also were odered there by them for my accomodation; among which a handsome 8 oared barge rowed by 8 American Captns. attended. In my way down the River I called upon Mrs. Green the Widow of the deceased Genl. Green, (at a place called Mulberry Grove) and asked her how she did. At this place (2 miles from Puris-

36

burgh) my horses and Carriages were landed, and had 12 miles farther by Land to Savanna. The wind and tide being both agst. us, it was 6 o'clock before we reached the City where we were received under every demonstration that could be given of joy and respect.

Sunday, May 15th.
After morning Service, and receiving a number of visits from the most respectable ladies of the place (as was the case yesterday) I set out for Augusta, Escorted beyd. the limits of the City by most of the Gentlemen in it, and dining at Mulberry Grove the Seat of Mrs. Green, lodged at one Spencers—distant 15 miles.

Savanna stands upon what may be called high ground for this Country. It is extremely Sandy wch. makes the walking very disagreeable; and the houses uncomfortable in warm and windy weather, as they are filled with dust whenever these happen. The town on 3 sides is surrounded with cultivated Rice fields which have a rich and luxuriant appearance.

Thursday, May 19th.
Received and answered an Address from the Citizens of Augusta; dined with a large Company of them at their Court Ho. and went to an Assembly in the evening at the Accadamy; at which there were between 60 and 70 well dressed ladies.

Sunday, May 22nd.
Rode about 21 miles to breakfast, and passing through the village of Granby just below the first falls in the Congaree (which was passed in a flat bottomed boat at a Rope ferry,) I lodged at Columbia, the newly adopted Seat of the Government of South Carolina about 3 miles from it, on the No. side of the River, and 27 from my breakfasting stage.

The whole Road from Augusta to Columbia is a pine barren of the worst sort, being hilly as well as poor. This circumstance added to the distance, length of the stages, want of water and heat of the day, foundered one of my horses very badly.

Monday, May 30th.
The lands between Charlotte and Salisbury are very fine, of a reddish cast and well timbered, with but very little underwood.

Between these two places are the first meadows I have seen on the Road since I left Virga. and here also we appear to be getting into a Wheat Country.

Tuesday, June 7th.
Left Colo. Coles by day break, and breakfasted at Charlotte Ct. Ho. [Virginia] 15 miles where I was detained sometime to get shoes put on such horses as had lost them—proceeded afterwards to Prince Edward Court House 20 Miles further.

Sunday, June 12th.
About Sunrise we were off—breakfasted at Dumfries and arrived at Mt. Vn. to Dinr. From Monday 13th until Monday the 27th (being the day I had appointed to meet the Commissioners under the residence act, at Georgetown) I remained at home; and spent my time in daily rides to my severl. farms and in receiving many visits.

Tuesday, June 28th.
Whilst the Commissioners were engaged in preparing the Deeds to be signed by Subscribers this afternoon, I went out [from Georgetown] with Majr. L'Enfant and Mr. Ellicot to take a more perfect view of the ground, in order to decide finally on the spots on which to place the public buildings and to direct how a line which was to leave out a Spring (commonly known by the name of the Cool Spring) belonging to Majr. Stoddart should be run.

Monday, July 4th.
This being the Anniversary of American Independence and being kindly requested to do it, I agreed to halt here [at Lancaster, Pennsylvania] this day and partake of the entertainment which was preparing for the celebration of it.

LEWIS AND CLARK EXPEDITION

Between the formulation of President Jefferson's plan to find a transcontinental route for interoceanic trade and the Lewis and Clark Expedition's departure on May 14, 1804, one of the most important events in world history took place—the Louisiana Purchase. When Jefferson asked Congress on January 18, 1803, to appropriate $2500 to cover the cost of an expedition to find a practical land-water route to the Pacific, he was talking about territory which did not belong to the United States. Jefferson had already started negotiations to buy New Orleans and some surrounding lands from France. But he did not know that his ministers in France would soon accomplish the purchase of the entire Louisiana Territory.

So Jefferson's message to Congress was secret; it referred to the abundance of furs going into the trade of Canada and the desirability of establishing commerce all the way to the Pacific. But the official wording, to allay any outside suspicions, was to be "for the purpose of extending the external commerce of the United States."

Following are excerpts from the President's letter of instructions to Meriwether Lewis, as well as an excerpt from Lewis and Clark's journals.

To Meriwether Lewis, esquire, Captain of the 1st regiment of infantry of the United States of America:

Your situation as Secretary of the President of the United States has made you acquainted with the objects of my confidential message of Jan. 18, 1803, to the legislature. you have seen the act they passed, which, tho' expressed in general terms, was meant to sanction those objects, and you are appointed to carry them into execution.

Instruments for ascertaining by celestial observations the geography of the country thro' which you will pass, have already been provided. light articles for barter, & presents among the Indians, arms for your attendants, say for from 10 to 12 men, boats, tents, & other travelling apparatus, with ammunition, medicine, surgical instruments & provisions you will have prepared with such aids as the Secretary at War can yield in his department; & from him also you will recieve authority to engage among our troops, by voluntary agreement, the number of attendants above mentioned, over whom you, as their commanding officer are invested with all the powers the laws give in such a case.

The object of your mission is to explore the Missouri river, & such principal stream of it, as, by it's course & communication with the waters of the Pacific Ocean, may offer the most direct & practicable water communication across this continent, for the purposes of commerce.

Beginning at the mouth of the Missouri, you will take observations of latitude & longitude, at all remarkable points on the river, & especially at the mouths of rivers, at rapids, at islands & other places & objects distinguished by such natural marks & characters of a durable kind, as that they may with certainty be recognized hereafter. the courses of the river between these points of observation may be supplied by the compass, the log-line & by time, corrected by the observations themselves. the variations of the compass too, in different places, should be noticed.

The interesting points of the portage between the heads of the Missouri & the water offering the best communication with the Pacific Ocean should also be fixed by observation, & the course of that water to the ocean, in the same manner as that of the Missouri.

The commerce which may be carried on with the people inhabiting the line you will pursue, renders a knolege of these people important. you will therefore endeavor to make yourself acquainted, as far as a diligent pursuit of your journey shall admit,

with the names of the nations & their numbers; the extent & limits of their possessions; their relations with other tribes or nations; their language, traditions, monuments; their ordinary occupations in agriculture, fishing, hunting, war, arts, & the implements for these; their food, clothing, & domestic accomodations; the diseases prevalent among them, & the remedies they use; moral & physical circumstances which distinguish them from the tribes we know; peculiarities in their laws, customs & dispositions; and articles of commerce they may need or furnish, & to what extent.

And considering the interest which every nation has in extending & strengthening the authority of reason & justice among the people around them, it will be useful to acquire what knolege you can of the state of morality, religion & information among them, as it may better enable those who endeavor to civilize & instruct them, to adapt their measures to the existing notions & practises of those on whom they are to operate.

Other object worthy of notice will be the soil & face of the country, it's growth & vegetable productions; especially those not of the U.S. the animals of the country generally, & especially those not known in the U.S. the remains and accounts of any which may deemed rare or extinct; the mineral productions of every kind; but more particularly metals, limestone, pit coal & saltpetre; salines & mineral waters, noting the temperature of the last, & such circumstances as may indicate their character. Volcanic appearances. climate as characterized by the thermometer, by the proportion of rainy, cloudy & clear days, by lightening, hail, snow, ice, by the access & recess of frost, by the winds prevailing at different seasons, the dates at which particular plants put forth or lose their flowers, or leaf, times of appearance of particular birds, reptiles or insects.

In all your intercourse with the natives treat them in the most friendly & conciliatory manner which their own conduct will admit; allay all jealousies as to the object of your journey, satisfy them of it's innocence, make them acquainted with the position, extent, character, peaceable & commercial dispositions of the

U.S. of our wish to be neighborly, friendly & useful to them, & of our dispositions to a commercial intercourse with them; confer with them on the points most convenient as mutual emporiums, & the articles of most desireable interchange for them &, us. if a few of their influential chiefs, within practicable distance, wish to visit us, arrange such a visit with them, and furnish them with authority to call on our officers, on their entering the U.S. to have them conveyed to this place at public expence. if any of them should wish to have some of their young people brought up with us, & taught such arts as may be useful to them, we will receive, instruct & take care of them. such a mission, whether of influential chiefs, or of young people, would give some security to your own party. carry with you some matter of the kine-pox, inform those of them with whom you may be of it' efficacy as a preservative from the small-pox; and instruct & encourage them in the use of it. This may be especially done wherever you winter.

As it is impossible for us to foresee in what manner you will be recieved by those people, whether with hospitality or hostility, so is it impossible to prescribe the exact degree of perseverance with which you are to pursue your journey. we value too much the lives of citizens to offer them to probably destruction. your numbers will be sufficient to secure you against the unauthorised opposition of individuals, or of small parties: but if a superior force, authorised or not authorised, by a nation, should be arrayed against your further passage, & inflexibly determined to arrest it, you must decline it's further pursuit, and return. in the loss of yourselves, we should lose also the information you will have acquired. by returning safely with that, you may enable us to renew the essay with better calculated means. to your own discretion therefore must be left the degree of danger you may risk, & the point at which you should decline, only saying we wish you to err on the side of your safety, & bring back your party safe, even if it be with less information.

Should you reach the Pacific ocean inform yourself of the circumstances which may decide whether the furs of those parts may not be collected as advantageously at the head of the Missouri (convenient as is supposed to the waters of the Colorado & Oregon or Columbia) as at Nootka sound or any other point of that coast; & that trade be consequently conducted through the Missouri & U.S. more beneficially than by the circumnavigation now practised.

On your arrival on that coast endeavor to learn if there by any port within your reach frequented by the sea-vessels of any nation, and to send two of your trusty people back by sea, in such way as shall appear practicable, with a copy of your notes. and should you be of opinion that the return of your party by the way they went will be eminently dangerous, then ship the whole, & return by sea by way of Cape Horn or the Cape of good Hope, as you shall be able. as you will be without money, clothes or provision, you must endeavor to use the credit of the U.S. to obtain them; for which purpose open letters of credit shall be furnished you authorising you to draw on the Executive of the U.S. or any of its officers in any part of the world, on which drafts can be disposed of, and to apply with our recommendations to the Consuls, agents, merchants or citizens of any nation with which we have intercourse, assuring them in our name that any aids they may furnish you, shall honorably repaid, and on demand. Our consuls Thomas Howes at Batavia in Java, William Buchanan of the isles of France and Bourbon, & John Elmslie at the Cape of good hope will be able to supply your necessities by draughts on us.

To provide, on the accident of your death, against anarchy, dispersion & the consequent danger to your party, and total failure of the enterprise, you are hereby authorised, by any instrument signed & written in your hand, to name the person among them who shall succeed to the command on your decease, & by like instruments to change the nomination from time to time, as further experience of the characters accompanying you shall point out superior fitness: and all the powers & authorities given to yourself are, in the event of your death, transferred to & vested in the successor so named, with further power to him, & his successors in like manner to name each his successor, who, on the death of his predecessor, shall be invested with all the powers & authorities given to yourself.

Given under my hand at the city of Washington, this 20th day of June 1803

Th. Jefferson
Pr. U.S. of America

43

The following account is from Lewis' entry in his diary for Tuesday, May 14, 1805.

One of the party wounded a brown [grizzly] bear very badly, but being alone did not think proper to pursue him. In the evening the men in two of the rear canoes discovered a large brown bear lying in the open grounds about 300 paces from the river, and six of them went out to attack him, all good hunters; they took the advantage of a small eminence which concealed them and got within 40 paces of him unperceived, two of them reserved their fires as had been previously conscerted, the four others fired nearly at the same time and put each his bullet through him, two of the balls passed through the bulk of both lobes of his lungs, in an instant this monster ran at them with open mouth, the two who had reserved their fir[e]s discharged their pieces at him as he came towards them, boath of them struck him, one only slightly and the other fortunately broke his shoulder, this however only retarded his motion for a moment only, the men unable to reload their guns took to flight, the bear pursued and had very nearly overtaken them before they reached the river; two of the party betook themselves to a canoe and the others separated an[d] concealed themselves among the willows, reloaded their pieces, each discharged his piece at him as they had an opportunity they struck him several times again but the guns served only to direct the bear to them, in this manner he pursued two of them separately so close that they were obliged to throw aside their guns and pouches and throw themselves into the river altho' the bank was nearly twenty feet perpendicular; so enraged was this anamal that he plunged into the river only a few feet behind the second man he had compelled [to] take refuge in the water, when one of those who still remained on shore shot him through the head and finally killed him; they then took him on shore and butch[er]ed him when they found eight balls had passed through him in different directions; the bear being old the flesh was indifferent, they therefore only took the skin and fleece, the latter made us several gallons of oil.

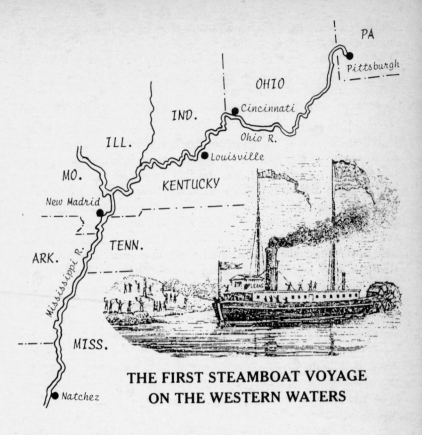

THE FIRST STEAMBOAT VOYAGE
ON THE WESTERN WATERS

Robert Fulton, designer of the first commercially-successful steamboat, and his financial backer, Robert Livingston, were not content to operate within the narrow confines of the Hudson River, where Livingston controlled the steamboat business through a monopoly obtained from the New York legislature. They foresaw the churning paddle wheel bringing commerce to the watercourses of the vast mid-Western wilderness, and they intended to be in on the ground floor there, too, so to speak. In 1809, two years after steam navigation was inaugurated on the Hudson, they felt they were ready to seek wider opportunities beyond the Appalachian Mountains. Their first move was to send 41-year-old Nicholas J. Roosevelt to investigate the inland waters.

Newly married, Roosevelt combined his survey of the Western rivers with a honeymoon trip—in what was probably the plushest flatboat ever seen. His bride was Lydia Latrobe, a teen-age daughter of noted architect Benjamin Henry Latrobe. Starting at Pittsburgh, the couple floated with the current some 2,000 miles down the Ohio and Mississippi. They were especially interested in coal deposits they saw along the Ohio. Indeed, at several places Roosevelt had the coal seams worked and fuel piled on the river bank in anticipation of the steamboat's advent.

On the strength of their scout's findings, Fulton and Livingston decided to build a steamboat on the Monongahela in western Pennsylvania. Roosevelt, whose brother James was to become the great grandfather of the famous "Teddy," directed the construction of both the hull and the engine for the boat, which they named the New Orleans. A bit over 100 feet long, with a beam of about 20 feet, she was designed along the lines of Fulton's Hudson River creations—long, narrow side-wheelers with considerable draft, too much draft, in fact, for the sandbars and shifting, shallow channels of the meandering Mississippi. Nevertheless, one day late in September of 1811 her commander, the intrepid Roosevelt, nosed her into the down-stream current at Pittsburgh and gave a "goodbye" toot on his whistle. Mrs. Roosevelt, who was expecting her second child, was on board.

The Roosevelts never put their unusual experiences on paper. But years later, while Mrs. Roosevelt was still alive and able to check the story, her brother, J. H. B. Latrobe, wrote a fascinating account of the trip, from which the following is excerpted. It first appeared in print in a publication of the Maryland Historical Society for October 1871.

There were two cabins, one aft, for ladies, and a larger one forward for gentlemen. In the former there were four berths. It was comfortably furnished. Of this, Mrs. Roosevelt took possession. Mr. Roosevelt and herself were the only passengers. There was a captain, an engineer named Baker, Andrew Jack, the pilot, six hands, two female servants, a man waiter, a cook, and an immense Newfoundland dog, named Tiger. Thus equipped, the *New Orleans* began the voyage which changed the relations of the West—which may almost be said to have changed its destiny.

On the second day after leaving Pittsburg, the *New Orleans* rounded to opposite Cincinnati, and cast anchor in the stream. Levees and wharf boats were things unknown in 1811. Here, as at Pittsburg, the whole town seemed to have assembled on the bank, and many of the acquaintances of the former visit came off in small boats. "Well, you are as good as your word; you have visited us in a steamboat," they said; "but we see you for the last time. Your boat may go *down* the river; but, as to coming up it, the very idea is an absurd one."

The stay at Cincinnati was brief, only long enough to take in a supply of wood for the voyage to Louisville, which was reached on the night of the fourth day after leaving Pittsburg. It was midnight on the first of October, 1811, that the *New Orleans* dropped anchor opposite the town. There was a brilliant moon. It was as light as day almost, and no one on board had retired. The roar of the escaping steam, then heard for the first time at the place where now its echoes are unceasing, roused the population, and, late as it was, crowds came rushing to the bank of the river to learn the cause of the unwonted uproar. A letter now before me, written by one of those on board at the time, records the fact—that there were those who insisted that the comet of 1811 had fallen into the Ohio and had produced the hubbub!

It had been intended, on leaving Pittsburg, to proceed as rapidly as possible to New Orleans, to place the boat on the route for which it was designed, between that city and Natchez. It was found, however, on reaching Louisville, that there was not a sufficient depth of water on the Falls of the Ohio to permit the vessel to pass over them in safety. Nothing was to be done, therefore, but to wait, as patiently as possible, for a rise in the river. That this delay might, as far as practicable, be utilized to the extent, at least, of convincing incredulous Cincinnatians, the *New Orleans* returned to that city, where she was greeted with an enthusiasm that exceeded even what was displayed on her descent from Pittsburg. No one doubted now.

Returning to Louisville, the great interest of all on board the *New Orleans* centered in watching the rise in the Ohio. Rain in the upper country was what was wanted, and of this there seemed small promise.

At last, and when a nervous impatience affected every one on board, it was announced one morning that there had been a rise in the river during the night. There was another announcement of a very different character. Mrs. Roosevelt had, for the second time, become a mother. The events of the voyage were certainly multiplying. Fortunately, this addition to the passengers happened when the *New Orleans* was necessarily detained in port.

Morning after morning, the rise in the river during the night was reported; and finally, in the last week of November, it was ascertained that the depth of water in the shallowest portion of the Falls exceeded by five inches the draught of the boat. It was a narrow margin. But the rise had ceased; there was no telegraph in those days to tell hourly what was the weather in the country drained by the Ohio; and Mr. Roosevelt, assuring himself personally of the condition of the Falls, determined to take the responsibility and go over them if he could. It was an anxious time. All hands were on deck. Mrs. Roosevelt, whom her husband would willingly have left behind to join him below the Falls, refused to remain on shore, and stood near the stern. The two pilots, for an extra one had been engaged for the passage through the rapids, took their places in the bow. The anchor was weighed. To get into the Indiana channel, which was the best, a wide circuit had to be made bringing her head downstream, completing which the *New Orleans* began the descent. Steerage way depended upon her speed exceeding that of the current. The faster she could be made to go, the easier it would be to guide her. All the steam the boiler would bear was put upon her. The safety valve shrieked; the wheels revolved faster than they had ever done before; and the vessel, speaking figuratively, fairly flew away from the crowds collected to witness her departure from Louisville.

Instinctively, each one on board now grasped the nearest object, and with bated breath awaited the result. Black ledges of rock appeared only to disappear as the *New Orleans* flashed by them. The waters whirled and eddied and threw their spray upon the deck, as a more rapid descent caused the vessel to pitch forward to what at times seemed inevitable destruction. Not a word was spoken. The pilots directed the men at the helm by motions of their hands. Even the great Newfoundland dog seemed affected by the apprehension of danger, and came and crouched at Mrs. Roosevelt's feet. The tension on the nervous system was too great to be long sustained. Fortunately, the

48

passage was soon made; and, with feelings of profound gratitude to the Almighty at the successful issue of the adventure, on the part of both Mr. Roosevelt and his wife, the *New Orleans* rounded to in safety below the Falls.

Hitherto the voyage had been one of pleasure. Nothing had marred the enjoyment of the travelers. The receptions at Louisville and Cincinnati had been great events. But now were to come, to use the words of the letter already referred to, "those days of horror." The comet of 1811 had disappeared, and was followed by the earthquake of that year, of which the atmospheric phenomena just mentioned were prognostics; and the earthquake accompanied the *New Orleans* far on her way down the Mississippi.

The first shock that was observed was felt on board the *New Orleans* while she lay at anchor after passing the Falls. The effect was as though the vessel had been in motion and had suddenly grounded. The cable shook and trembled, and many on board experienced for the moment a nausea resembling sea sickness. It was a little while before they could realize the presence of the dread visitor. It was wholly unexpected. The shocks succeeded each other during the night. When morning came, the voyage was resumed; and while under way, the jar of the machinery, the monotonous beating of the wheels and the steady progress of the vessel prevented the disturbance from being noticed.

It has already been mentioned that, in his voyage of exploration, Mr. Roosevelt had found coal on the Ohio and that he had caused mines to be opened in anticipation. Their value was now realized; and, when he reached them on his way down the river, he took on board as much coal as he could find room for.

Some miles above the mouth of the Ohio, the diminished speed of the current indicated a rise in the Mississippi. This was found to be the case. The bottom lands on either shore were under water, and there was every sign of an unwonted flood. Canoes came and went among the boles of the trees. Sometimes the Indians attempted to approach the steamboat; and, again, fled on its approach. The Chickasaws still occupied that part of the State of Tennessee lying below the mouth of the Ohio. On one occasion, a large canoe, fully manned, came out of the woods abreast of the steamboat. The Indians, outnumbering the crew of the vessel, paddled after it. There was at once a race, and for a time the contest was equal. The result, however, was what might have been anticipated. Steam had the advantage of endurance; and the Indians with wild shouts, which might have been shouts of defiance, gave up the pursuit, and turned into the forest from whence they had emerged.

Early in the afternoon of each day, the steamer was rounded to and fastened to the bank, the crew going ashore to cut the wood required, after the coal was exhausted, for the next day's consumption. On some of these occasions, squatters came on board with tales of their experiences upon the land, which they insisted shook and trembled under their feet. At New Madrid [Missouri], a great portion of which had been engulfed, as the earth opened in vast chasms and swallowed up houses and their inhabitants, terror-stricken people had begged to be taken on board, while others, dreading the steamboat even more than the earthquake, hid themselves as she approached.

One of the peculiar characteristics of the voyage was the silence that prevailed on board. No one seemed disposed to talk; and when there was any conversation, it was carried on in whispers, almost. Tiger, who appeared alone to be aware of the earthquake while the vessel was in motion, prowled about, moaning and growling; and when he came and placed his head on Mrs. Roosevelt's lap, it was a sure sign of a commotion of more than usual violence. Orders were given in low tones; and the usual cheerful "aye, aye, sir" of the sailors was almost inaudible. Sleeplessness was another characteristic. Sound, continuous sleep was apparently unknown.

Nor was this depression confined to the steamer. Flatboats and barges were passed, whose crews, instead of bandying river wit, as they had done when met on the voyage from Pittsburg to Louisville, uttered no word as the *New Orleans* went by. Before the travelers had been many days on the Mississippi, they fancied, as they looked at each other, that they had become haggard. Mrs. Roosevelt records "that she lived in a constant fright, unable to sleep or sew or read."

Sometimes Indians would join the wood choppers; and occasionally one would be able to converse in English with the men. From these it was learned that the steamboat was called the "Penelore" or "Fire Canoe" and was supposed to have some affinity with the Comet that had preceded the earthquake—the sparks from the chimney of the boat being likened to the train of the celestial visitant. Again they would attribute the smoky atmosphere to the steamer, and the rumbling of the earth to the beating of the waters by the fast revolving paddles.

In the first part of the voyage when the steamboat rounded to at night, she was made fast to the river bank; but when it was seen that trees would occasionally topple and fall over, as the ground beneath them was shaken or gave way, it was thought safer to stop at the foot of an island, which might serve as a breakwater, taking care the trees were far enough from the boat to obviate apprehension from them. Once, however, when such a fastening had been made and a plank carried ashore and the wood chopping had been finished at an earlier hour than usual, a new experience was had. No shock had been felt during the day, and Mrs. Roosevelt anticipated a quiet rest. In this, however, she was disappointed. All night long she was disturbed by the jar and noise produced by hard objects grating against the planking outside the boat. At times severe blows were struck that caused the vessel to tremble through its entire length. Then there would follow a continuous scratching mingled with the gurgling sound of water. Driftwood had caused sounds of the same sort before, and it was thought that driftwood was again busy in producing them. With morning, however, came the true explanation. The island had disappeared; and it was the disintegrated fragments sweeping down the river that had struck the vessel from time to time and caused the noises that Mrs. Roosevelt had been disturbed by. At first, it was supposed that the *New Orleans* had been borne along by the current; but the pilot pointed to landmarks on the banks which proved that it was the island that had disappeared while the steamboat had kept its place. Where the island had been, there was now a broad reach of the river; and when the hawser was cut, for it was found impossible otherwise to free the vessel, the pilot was utterly at a loss which way to steer. Some flatboats were hailed, but they, too, were lost. Their main effort was, by dint of their long oars, to keep where the current was the strongest. This was evidently the best plan for the *New Orleans*.

As the *New Orleans* descended the river it passed out of the region of the earthquake, and the principal inconvenience was the number of shoals and snags and sawyers. These were all safely passed, however, and the vessel came in sight of Natchez, and rounded to opposite the landing place. Expecting to remain here for a day or two, the engineer had allowed his fires to go down, so that when the boat turned its head up stream it lost headway altogether and was being carried down by the current far below the intended landing. Thousands were assembled on the bluff and at the foot of it; and for a moment it would have seemed that the *New Orleans* had achieved what she had done, so far, only that she might be overcome at last. Fresh fuel, however, was added—the engine was stopped that steam might accumulate, presently the safety valve lifted—a few turns of the wheels steadied the boat—a few more gave her headway; and, overcoming even the Mississippi, she gained the shore amid shouts of exultation and applause.

The romance of the voyage ended at Natchez, where the same hospitalities were extended to Mr. and Mrs. Roosevelt that had been enjoyed at Louisville. From thence to New Orleans, there was no occurrence worthy of note.

In a footnote, author Latrobe explained that his use of the word "romance" had a double meaning. The captain of the New Orleans *having fallen in love with Mrs. Roosevelt's maid, the first order of business at Natchez was a wedding. Whether the pair lived happily ever after, he failed to state. As for the later career of the little steamer, she was put into service on the short, smooth stretch of the lower river between Natchez and New Orleans and soon was joined by several other craft designed by Robert Fulton. But "Ol Man River" did not really come alive until Henry M. Shreve, for whom Shreveport, Louisiana is named, began building the true Mississippi steamboat — the flat–bottomed, snub-nosed, puffing two-stacker of story and song.*

In America there are two classes of travel—first class, and with children.

—Robert Benchley

FROM "A HISTORY OF ROADS"

Turnpikes and toll roads have carried America's travelers for almost two hundred years. The following excerpt from A HISTORY OF ROADS, *by Geoffrey Hindley, relates some interesting facts about our first hard-surfaced roads.*

In the matter of road-building the colonial government followed the policy of the mother country and did nothing. The inheritance of the new nation was limited to the Cumberland road laid out by Braddock. Americans of the colonial period were probably familiar with the principle of the turnpike from English example, but the first American turnpike was a state enterprise launched by Virginia. This was opened only in 1785 and it was not until the 1790s, when private companies began to operate, that the movement gathered strength.

In 1794 the Philadelphia-Lancaster turnpike opened; it had an overall width of thirty-seven feet, a stone and gravel surface twenty-four feet wide and was the first major paved road in North America. Serving a prosperous agricultural region, it rapidly showed considerable profits.

By the mid 1820s such roads with their toll-gates were a common sight all over the eastern states. Among the better-known were the roads from Boston to New York, from New York to Albany, one on either side of the Hudson river, and the roads westward from Albany to Buffalo. The great period of the turnpikes was the first forty years of the century, and the traffic that used them ranged from stage coaches to droves of horses, sheep and cattle.

During their heyday the turnpikes amply repaid the expenses of their building. Toll-gates at intervals of between six and ten miles levied rates of up to 25 cents per vehicle so that, for example, to travel the whole length of the Lancaster pike through its nine gates might cost a wagoner as much as $2.25. But the service was well worth the charge as generally these roads were well built and maintained. With the development of the canal, and above all the railway network, they rapidly lost custom.

LOW BRIDGE,
EVERYBODY DOWN

Although the 363-mile Erie Canal, opened between Albany and Buffalo in 1825, brought great prosperity to New York State, for numerous foreign traveler-diarists its main function seemed to be to provide an unusual form of exercise—constantly ducking or flattening themselves on the deck (the roof of the boat) at the steersman's almost continual cry of "Bridge!" One such was young Carl David Arfwedson from Sweden, who also found the sleeping arrangements on horse-drawn canal boats of 1832 a bit odd, and precarious.

On returning to Schenectady, I availed myself of a canal-boat on the point of starting for Utica. These boats are generally very long, but low, in consequence of the many bridges thrown across the canal, beneath which they must pass. They are fitted up with two rooms, one inside the other, taking up the whole length of the boat, with small windows on the sides. The inner room belonged exclusively to the ladies, and was considered as a sanctuary into which the profane dared not set foot; the outer one again was used both as a drawing, dining, and bed room for the gentlemen. When—as was the case now—the number of travellers exceeded thirty, and the majority belonged to the stronger sex, the prospect of remaining on board twenty-two hours was not very agreeable. It was impossible either to walk, to sit, or to lie. Moving about upon deck was out of the question, owing to the number of bridges beneath which we had to pass; at every passage it became necessary for the whole company to lie down flat, to avoid being swept away by the beams of the bridge. As soon as we approached one, which happened every five minutes, the steersman called out, "Bridge!" and at the same instant the company fell prostrate. It was ludicrous for a while to take part in this manœuvre; in the long run, however, it became wearisome, and no other alternative was left but to go down, by way of change, into the close and narrow cabin.

Night made our situation still more uncomfortable. Although three tiers of beds, one above another, had been fitted up on the sides, their number proved insufficient; the floor was covered with mattresses. Had I been permitted to select a sleeping place, I should unquestionably have preferred a mattress on the floor, for the beds on the sides were only slung by a cord to the top: had that given way the whole sleeping apparatus would have been precipitated to the ground; and the consequences might have been serious, from the corpulence of some of the travellers. Unfortunately, nearly all had the same idea as myself. The captain, a peaceable man, wishing to accommodate every one, saw that it was not in his power to do so, except by drawing lots for the births. I drew my number with a trembling hand, and behold! it turned out to be one of the lowest beds on the side. The prospect now darkened indeed: to lie down, having two other births occupied by heavy inmates above, and only supported by small cords, was a prospect by no means enviable. But what was to be done? I had no other chance but quietly to take my place, unless I chose to spend the night on deck; and this was still more objectionable, owing to a heavy rain which continued till the following morning. I thought it prudent, however, to enter into a convention with the occupants of the upper regions, stipulating that they should remain quiet in their births, and that, if a change of position became absolutely necessary, they should inform me beforehand of their intention, to guard against the possibility of accidents. Immediately above me lay a young man, and above him rested an excessively corpulent man, whose frame took up more room than was allotted to two.

The beginning of the night was rather auspicious: I already

felt reconciled to my unpleasant situation, and amused myself by listening to the different sounds, from the finest tenor to the strongest bass, proceeding from the snoring gentry. A sudden thump against my side of the boat at length spread consternation among the travellers. The shock, occasioned by another craft coming too close to ours, was so violent, that the beams cracked, and the doors flew open. About a dozen sleeping individuals were precipitated from the second and third tier on the unfortunate beings who were lying on the floor. One cord gave way after another. Snoring had ceased: lamentations filled the room. The ladies rushed in among us. All were running, shoving against each other, swearing, and making a noise in the dark: confusion, in short, was at its height, until the captain had made a favourable report, which restored tranquillity. The births were soon re-occupied.

The turn-of-the-century traveler arriving in Texas for the first time encountered a brand of humor peculiar to residents of that state. Texans told fantastic stories about the beauties of their land, but they also bragged about the bad things. Their rivers were the dustiest, their droughts the driest. This story, retold by Mody C. Boatright in *Folk Laughter on the American Frontier*, gives a good picture of Texas mud:

A man was struggling to get through an especially muddy stretch of country road when he saw a hat lying on the ground. It looked like a pretty good hat and he dismounted to pick it up. Leaning out cautiously over the mudhole, he seized it by the crown and a voice from beneath called out, "Hey, what you doing there?" The hat was on a man's head.

"Do you need any help?" the wearer was asked.

"No, thank you," he replied. "I'm riding a mighty good horse and I guess I'll make it through."

EARLY MISSIONARY TRAVEL IN HAWAII

Modern-day travelers viewing the scenic wonders of the Fiftieth State have few worries about transportation. For the early missionaries who came to the Sandwich Islands to preach Christianity to the natives, the exact opposite was the rule. Connecticut-born Reverend Titus Coan, a Presbyterian who began his 47-year ministry to the Hilo district of the island of Hawaii in 1835, found that he not only had to be a tireless and sure-footed hiker, but a nimble pole-vaulter, a fearless equestrian, and an expert sailor. His harrowing experiences while tending his flock are described in his autobiography, LIFE IN HAWAII, *published in 1882.*

In passing through the district of Hilo, the weather was sometimes fine and the rivers low, so that there was little difficulty in traveling. The path was a simple trail, winding in a serpentine line, going down and up precipices, some of which could only be descended and ascended by grasping the shrubs and grasses, and with no little weariness and difficulty and some danger.

But the streams were the most formidable obstacles. In great rains, which often occurred on my tours, when the winds rolled in the heavy clouds from the sea, and massed them in dark banks on the side of the mountain, the waters would fall in torrents at the head of the streams and along their channels, and the rush and the roar as the floods came down were like the thunder of an army charging upon the foe.

I have sometimes sat on the high bank of a streamlet, not more than fifteen to twenty feet wide, conversing with natives in the bright sunshine, when suddenly a portentous roaring, "Like the sound of many waters, or like the noise of the sea when the waves thereof roar," fell upon my ears, and looking up-stream, I have seen a column of turbid waters six feet deep coming down like the flood from a broken mill-dam. The natives would say to me, *"Awiwi! awiwi! o paa oe i ka wai"*—"Quick! quick! or the waters will stop you."

Rushing down the bank I would cross over, dry-shod, where in two minutes more there was no longer any passage for man or beast. But I rarely waited for the rivers to run by. My appointments for preaching were all sent forward in a line for thirty or sixty miles, designating the day, and usually the hours, when I would be at a given station, and by breaking one of these links the whole chain would be disturbed. It therefore seemed important that every appointment should be kept, whatever the inconvenience might be to me.

I had several ways of crossing the streams.

1st. When the waters were low, large rocks and boulders, common in all the water-channels, were left bare, so that with a stick or pole eight or ten feet long, I leaped from rock to rock over the giddy streams and crossed dry-shod: these same poles helping me to climb up, and to let myself down steep precipices, and to leap ditches six to eight feet wide. 2d. When the streams were not too deep and too swift I waded them; and 3d, when not too deep, but too swift, I mounted upon the shoulders of a sturdy aquatic native, holding on to his bushy hair, when he moved carefully down the slippery bank of the river, leaning up-stream against a current of ten knots, and moving one foot at a time, sideways among the slimy boulders in the bottom, and then bringing the other foot carefully up. Thus slowly feeling his way across, he would land me safe with a shout and a laugh on the opposite bank. But this is a fearful way of crossing, for the cataracts are so numerous, the waters so rapid, and the uneven bottom so slippery, that the danger of falling is imminent, and the recovery from a fall often impossible, the current hurrying one swiftly over a precipice into certain destruction.

I once crossed a full and powerful river in this way, not more than fifty feet above a cataract of 426 feet in height, with a basin forty feet deep below, where this little Niagara has thundered for ages. A missionary brother of another station seeing me landed safely, and knowing that this crossing would save about six miles of hard and muddy walking, followed me on the shoulders of the same bold native that took me over. But before he had reached the middle of the rushing flood, he trembled and cried out with fear. The bearer said, "Hush! hush! be still, or we perish together." The brother still trembling, the native with great difficulty managed to reach a rock in the center of the river, and on this he seated his burden, commanding him to be quiet and sit there until he was cool (he was already drenched with rain and river-spray), when he would take him off, which he did in about ten minutes and landed him safely by my side.

This mode of crossing the streams, however, was too dangerous, and I soon abandoned it.

A fourth mode was for a sufficient number of strong men to form a chain across the river. They made a line, locking hands on the bank; with heads bending up-stream entering the water carefully, and moving slowly until the head of the line reached good foothold near the opposite bank. With my hands upon the shoulders of the men I passed along this chain of bones, sinews, and muscles and arrived in safety on the other side.

The fifth and safest, and in fact the only possible way to cross some of these rivers when swollen and raging, was to throw a rope across the stream, and fasten it to trees or rocks on either side; grasping it firmly with both hands, my feet thrown down-stream, I drew myself along the line and gained the opposite bank. This I sometimes did without removing shoes or garments, then walked on to my next station, and preached in wet clothes, continuing my travels and labors until night.

After years had passed, and a little had been done toward making roads, I purchased a horse, and tried to get him over these streams by swimming or hauling him over with ropes. Twice when I attempted to go over in the saddle, his foot caught between two rocks in the middle of the stream, and horse and rider were saved only by the energy and fidelity of the natives.

Once in going up a steep precipice in a narrow pass between a rocky height on one hand and a stream close on the other, my horse fell over backward and lay with his head down and his feet in the air, so wedged and so wounded that he could never have escaped from his position, had not a company of natives for whom I sent came [sic] to the rescue and extricated the poor, faithful animal from his rocky bed. I escaped instant death by sliding out of the saddle upon the narrow bank of the stream, before the back of my horse struck between the rocks. He was so hurt that I was obliged to leave him to recover.

In order to save time and escape the weariness of the road and the dangers of the rivers, I sometimes took a canoe at the end of my tours to return home by the water. This trip required six to eight hours, and was usually made in the night.

On three occasions my peril was great. One description will suffice for all; for although the difficulties and escapes were at different points along a precipitous and lofty sea-wall, yet the causes of danger were the same, viz.: stormy winds, raging billows, and want of landing-places.

About midway between our starting-place and Hilo harbor, we were met by a strong head-wind, with pouring rain and tumultuous waves in a dark midnight. We were half a mile from land, but could hear the roar and see the flashing of the white surf as it dashed against the rocky walls. We could not land, we could not sail, we could not row forward or backward. All we could do was to keep the prow of the canoe to the wind, and bail. Foaming seas dashed against our frail cockleshell, pouring in buckets of brine. Thus we lay about five hours, anxious as they "who watch for the morning." At length it dawned; we looked through the misty twilight to the rock-bound shore where "the waves dashed high." A few doors of native huts opened and men crawled out. We called, but no echo came. We made signals of distress. We were seen and numbers came down to the cliffs and gazed at us. We waved our garments for them to come off to our help. They feared, they hesitated. We were opposite the mouth of a roaring river, where the foam of breakers dashed in wild fury. At last four naked men came down from the cliff, plunged into the sea, dived under one towering wave after another, coming out to breathe between the great rolling billows, and thus reached our canoe. Ordering the crew to swim to the land, they took charge of the canoe themselves because they knew the shore. Meanwhile men stood on the high cliffs with kapa cloth in hand to signal to the boat-men when to strike for the mouth of the river. They waited long and watched the tossing waves as they rolled in and thundered upon the shore, and when at last a less furious wave came behind us, the shore men waved the signals and cried out, *"Hoi! hoi!"* and as the waves lifted the stern of our canoe, all the paddles struck the water, while the steerer kept the canoe straight on her course, and thus mounted on this crested wave as on an ocean chariot, with the feathery foam flying around us, we rode triumphantly into the mouth of the river, where we were received with shouts of gladness by the throng who had gathered to witness our escape. Then two rows of strong men waded into the surf up to their arm-pits to receive our canoe and bear it in triumph to the shore . . .

STEAMBOATING WITH CHARLES DICKENS

Like nearly everything else he saw in raw, youthful America, Ohio River steamboats of 1842 were a great disappointment, and a bit frightening, to visiting English novelist Charles Dickens. As the elegant and graceful white river packets of the Currier & Ives prints were still a decade in the future, in journeying from Pittsburgh to St. Louis Dickens and his wife had to put up with grubby, crowded craft and, to them, unpalatable table fare. The trip, described in AMERICAN NOTES, *necessitated changing boats at Cincinnati and Louisville. Here are one Englishman's impressions of his first inland river steamboat, the* Messenger, *and her passengers.*

The *Messenger* was one among a crowd of high-pressure steamboats, clustered together by the wharf-side, which, looked down upon from the rising ground that forms the landing-place, and backed by the lofty bank on the opposite side of the river, appeared no larger than so many floating models. She had some forty passengers on board, exclusive of the poorer persons on the lower deck; and in half an hour, or less, proceeded on her way.

We had, for ourselves, a tiny state-room with two berths in it, opening out of the ladies' cabin. There was undoubtedly something satisfactory in this "location," inasmuch as it was in the stern, and we had been a great many times very gravely recommended to keep as far aft as possible, "because the steamboats generally blew up forward." Nor was this an unnecessary caution, as the occurrence and circumstances of more than one such fatality during our stay sufficiently testified. Apart from this source of self-congratulation, it was an unspeakable relief to have any place, no matter how confined, where one could be alone; and as the row of little chambers of which this was one, had each a second glass-door besides that in the ladies' cabin, which opened on a narrow gallery outside the vessel, where the other passengers seldom came, and where one could sit in peace and gaze upon the shifting prospect, we took possession of our new quarters with much pleasure.

If the native packets I have already described be unlike anything we are in the habit of seeing on water, these Western vessels are still more foreign to all the ideas we are accustomed to entertain of boats. I hardly know what to liken them to, or how to describe them.

In the first place, they have no mast, cordage, tackle, rigging, or other such boat-like gear; nor have they anything in their shape at all calculated to remind one of a boat's head, stern, sides, or keel. Except that they are in the water, and display a couple of paddle-boxes, they might be intended, for anything that appears to the contrary, to perform some unknown service, high and dry, upon a mountain top. There is no visible deck, even: nothing but a long, black, ugly roof, covered with burnt-out feathery sparks; above which tower two iron chimneys, and a hoarse escape-valve, and a glass steerage-house. Then, in order as the eye descends towards the water, are the sides, and doors, and windows of the state-rooms, jumbled as oddly together as though they formed a small street, built by the varying tastes of a dozen men: the whole is supported on beams and pillars resting on a dirty barge, but a few inches above the water's edge: and in the narrow space between this upper structure and this barge's deck, are the furnace fires and machinery, open at the sides to every wind that blows, and every storm of rain it drives along its path.

Passing one of these boats at night, and seeing the great body of fire, exposed as I have just described, that rages and roars beneath the frail pile of painted wood: the machinery, not warded off or guarded in any way, but doing its work in the midst of the crowd of idlers and emigrants and children, who throng the lower deck; under the management, too, of reckless men whose acquaintance with its mysteries may have been of six months' standing: one feels directly that the wonder is, not that there should be so many fatal accidents, but that any journey should be safely made.

Within, there is one long narrow cabin, the whole length of the boat; from which the state-rooms open, on both sides. A small portion of it at the stern is partitioned off for the ladies; and the bar is at the opposite extreme. There is a long table down the centre, and at either end a stove. The washing apparatus is forward, on the deck.

We are to be on board the *Messenger* three days: arriving at Cincinnati (barring accidents) on Monday morning. There are three meals a day. Breakfast at seven, dinner at half-past twelve, supper about six. At each, there are a great many small dishes and plates upon the table, with very little in them; so that although there is every appearance of a mighty "spread," there is seldom really more than a joint: except for those who fancy slices of beetroot, shreds of dried beef, complicated entanglements of yellow pickle; maize, Indian corn, apple-sauce, and pumpkin.

Some people fancy all these little dainties together (and sweet preserves beside), by way of relish to their roast pig. They are generally those dyspeptic ladies and gentlemen who eat unheard-of quantities of hot corn-bread (almost as good for the digestion as a kneaded pin-cushion), for breakfast, and for supper. Those who do not observe this custom, and who help themselves several times instead, usually suck their knives and forks meditatively, until they have decided what to take next: then pull them out of their mouths; put them in the dish; help themselves; and fall to work again. At dinner, there is nothing to drink upon the table, but great jugs full of cold water. Nobody says anything, at any meal, to anybody.

It is quite a relief to have, sitting opposite, that little girl of fifteen with the loquacious chin: who, to do her justice, acts up to it, and fully identifies Nature's handwriting, for of all the small chatterboxes that ever invaded the repose of a drowsy ladies' cabin, she is the first and foremost. The beautiful girl, who sits a little beyond her—further down the table there—

married the young man with the dark whiskers, who sits beyond *her*, only last month. They are going to settle in the very Far West, where he has lived four years, but where she has never been. They were both overturned in a stage-coach the other day (a bad omen anywhere else, where overturns are not so common), and his head, which bears the marks of a recent wound, is bound up still. She was hurt too, at the same time, and lay insensible for some days; bright as her eyes are, now.

Further down still, sits a man who is going some miles beyond their place of destination, to "improve" a newly-discovered copper mine. He carries the village—that is to be—with him: a few frame cottages, and an apparatus for smelting the copper. He carries its people too. They are partly American and partly Irish, and herd together on the lower deck; where they amused themselves last evening till the night was pretty far advanced, by alternately firing off pistols and singing hymns.

They, and the very few who have been left at table twenty minutes, rise, and go away. We do so too; and passing through our little state-room, resume our seats in the quiet gallery without.

A fine broad river always, but in some parts much wider than in others: and then there is usually a green island, covered with trees, dividing it into two streams. Occasionally, we stop for a few minutes, maybe to take in wood, maybe for passengers, at some small town or village (I ought to say city, every place is a city here); but the banks are for the most part deep solitudes, overgrown with trees, which, hereabouts, are already in leaf and very green. For miles, and miles, and miles, these solitudes are unbroken by any sign of human life or trace of human footstep; nor is anything seen to move about them but the blue jay, whose colour is so bright, and yet so delicate, that it looks like a flying flower.

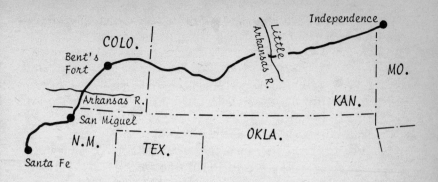

FIRST WOMAN TO CROSS THE PLAINS

A wagon train of fourteen wagons and twenty men headed westward from Independence, Missouri in June of 1846. The leader of the caravan, Santa Fe trader Samuel Magoffin, brought with him his eighteen-year-old bride Susan. For Susan, who had been raised on a large estate in Kentucky, the journey across the plains would be filled with adventure and many surprises. This is a portion of her diary of the trip westward.

June [1846]

From the city of New York to the Plains of Mexico is a stride that I myself can scarcely realize. Tuesday evening we went into Independence; there we stayed one night only at Mr. Noland's Hotel.

June 11th.

Now the Prairie life begins! We left "the settlements" this morning. Our mules travel well and we joged on at a rapid pace till 10 o'clock when we came up with the waggons.

We crossed the branch and stretched our tent. It is a grand affair indeed. 'Twas made in Philadelphia by a regular tentmaker of the army, and every thing is complete. Our bed is as good as many houses have; sheets, blankets, counterpanes, pillows &c. We have a carpet made of sail duck, have portable stools.

Well after a supper at *my own table* and in *my own house* I can say what few women in civilized life ever could, that the first house of his own to which my husband took me to after our

65

marriage was a *tent*, and the first table of my own at which I ever sat was a cedar one, made with only *one leg* and that was a tent pole.

June 12th.

At night we struck camp at "Black Jack," fourteen miles from the last, & 49 from Independence. Being tired of the carriage I got out and took a ramble.

I picked numberless flowers with which the plains are covered, and as *mi alma* [her term for her husband] told me before we started, I threw them away to gather more. I wearied myself out at this, and as the tent was now up, I returned *"home."*

There before supper I had a little piece of work to attend to, I mean the feeding of my chickens. It is quite a farm house this; poultry, dogs, cattle, mules, horses &c. Altogether my home is one not to be objected to.

June 14th.

This is my first sabbath on the plains!

A very quiet one it has been too, something I had not looked for. But all the men seem to recollect it and hitch in their teams with half the trouble, and I have scarcely heard an oath the whole day.

Noon. No. 20. Little Arkansas River. June 30th.

Now, about dark, we came into the musquito regions, and I found to my great *horror* that I have been complaining all this time for nothing, yes absolutely for *nothing*; for some two or hundred or even thousands are nothing compared with what we now encountered. The carriage mules became so restless that they passed all the wagons and swishing their tails from side to side, as fast as they could, and slaping their ears, required some strength of our Mexican driver to hold them in.

About 10 o'clock the mules became perfectly frantic, and nothing could make them stand. They were turned out to shift for themselves, and Magoffin seeing no other alternative than to remain there all night, tied his head and neck up with pocket handkerchiefs and set about having the tent stretched.

I drew my feet up under me, wraped my shawl over my head, till I almost smothered with heat, and listened to the din without. And such a noise as it was, I shall pray ever to be preserved. Millions upon millions were swarming around me,

66

and their knocking against the carriage *reminded me of a hard rain*. It was equal to any of the plagues of Egypt.

I lay almost in a perfect stupor, the heat and stings made me perfectly sick, till Magoffin came to the carriage and told me *to run if I could*, with my shawl, bonnet and shoes on (and without opening my mouth Jane said, for they would *choke* me) straight to bed.

When I got there they pushed me straight in under the musquito bar, which had been tied up in some kind of a fashion, and oh, dear, what a relief it was to breathe again. There I sat in my cage, like an imprisoned creature frightened half to death.

Magoffin now rolled himself up some how with all his clothes on, and lay down at my side, he dare not raise the bar to get in. I tried to sleep and towards daylight succeeded. On awakening this morning I found my forehead, arms and feet covered with knots as large as a pea.

July 6th. Camp No. 26.

It is a rich sight indeed to look at the fine fat [buffalo] meat stretched out on ropes to dry for our sustinence when we are no longer in the regions of the living animal. Such soup as we have made of the hump ribs, one of the most choice parts of the buffalo. I never eat its equal in the best hotels of N.Y. and Philada. And the sweetest butter and most delicate oil I ever tasted, 'tis not surpassed by the marrow taken from the thigh bones.

Mi alma was out this morning on a hunt, but I sincerely hope he will never go again. I am so uneasy from the start till he returns. There is danger attached to it that the excited hunter seldom thinks of till it overtake him. His horse may fall and kill him; the buffalo is apt too, to whirl suddenly on his persuer, and often serious if not fatal accidents occur. It is a painful situation to be placed in, to know that the being dearest to you on earth is in momentary danger of losing his life, or receiving for the remainder of his days, whether long or short, a tormenting wound.

July 30th.

Well this is my nineteenth birthday! And what? Why I feel rather strange, not surprised at its coming, nor to think that I am growing rather older, for that is the way of the human family, but this is it, I am sick! strange sensations in my head, my back and hips. I am obliged to lie down most of the time, and when I get up to hold my hand over my eyes.

There is the greatest possible noise in the *patio* [of Bent's Fort]. The shoeing of horses, neighing, and braying of mules, the crying of children, the scolding and fighting of men, are all enough to turn my head. And to add to the scene, like some of our neighbours we have our own private troubles. The servants are all quarreling and fighting among themselves, running to us to settle their difficulties; they are gambling off their cloths till some of them are next to nudity, and though each of them are in debt to *mi alma* for advancement of their wages, they are coming to him to get them out of their scrapes.

August, 1846. Thursday 6th.

The mysteries of a new world have been shown to me since last Thursday. In a few short months I should have been a happy mother and made the heart of a father glad, but the ruling hand of a mighty Providence has interposed and by an abortion deprived us of the hope.

My pains commenced and continued until 12 o'c. at night, when after much agony and severest of pains, which were relieved a little at times by medicine given by Dctr. Mesure, *all was over.* I sunk off into a kind of lethargy, in *mi alma's* arms. Since that time I have been in my bed till yesterday a little while, and a part of today.

My situation was very different from that of an Indian woman in the room below me. She gave birth to a fine healthy baby, about the same time, *and in half an hour after she went to the River and bathed herself and it,* and this she has continued every day since. Never could I have believed such a thing, if I had not been here, and *mi alma's* own eyes had not seen her coming from the River. And some gentlemen here tells him, he has often seen them immediately after the birth of a child go to the water and *break the ice* to bathe themselves!

Camp No.1. Saturday, August 8th. Second start.

The crossing of the Arkansas was an event in my life, I have never met with before; the separating me from my own dear native land. Perhaps I have left it for not only the first, but the last time.

August 24th. Camp No.18 Olla de Galinas.

Traveled late tonight and it has been so dark too, it was almost necessary to feel our way—with *mi alma's* careful driving though, I felt little fear.

How cheering it is to one when groping their way in the dark, over roads and through country he knew nothing about, all bewildered, and not knowing whether he is about pitching over a precipice, or driving into some deep ravine, whole, &c., to have the light of the camp fires of those ahead of them, to break suddenly before the eye. It is like drink to a thirsty traveler, or a straw to a drowning man.

August 27th. Near San Miguel.

We have passed through some two or three little settlements today and I am glad to think that much is accomplished of my task. It is truly shocking to my modesty to pass such places with gentlemen.

The women slap about with their arms and necks bare, perhaps their bosoms exposed (and they are none of the prettiest or whitest). If they are about to cross the little creek that is near all the villages, regardless of those about them, they pull their dresses, which in the first place but little more than cover their calves—up about their knees and paddle through the water like ducks, sloshing and spattering every thing about them.

Some of them wear leather shoes, from the States, but most have buckskin mockersins, Indian style.

And it is repulsive to see the children running about perfectly naked, or if they have on a chimese it is in such ribbands it had better be off at once. I am constrained to keep my veil drawn closely over my face all the time to protect my blushes.

Santa Fe. August 31st, 1846.

It is really hard to realize it, that I am here in my own house, in a place too where I once would have thought it folly to think of visiting. I have entered the city in a year that will always be remembered by my countrymen; and under the "Star-spangled banner" too, the first American lady, who has come under such auspices, and some of our company seem disposed to make me the first under any circumstances that ever crossed the Plains.

A MISSOURIAN IN THE GOLD RUSH

During the 1840's gold fever spread contagiously to those in quest of the American dream. A young, adventurous Missourian, Bennett C. Clark, quit his job and set out in 1849 with 23 other men to fulfill that dream. The romanticism of an overland journey in search of California gold was quickly dispelled, however, by his reports of "sterile lands and dust . . . the wolves . . . and sickness." Clark himself never reached the gold fields. He fell ill near Nevada's western border and had to be transported to San Francisco. From there he left for home by boat. Nevertheless, his diary reveals the tenacity and courage of America's early pioneers in overcoming overwhelming odds.

[May 3, 1849]

Finally we broke up our camp [at Westport, Missouri, now a part of Kansas City] and started on our long and toilsome journey.

May 6th.

Came up with a train of about forty wagons under the guidance of Capt. Hedgepeth, numbering in all about six hundred head of stock.

May 7th.

The camp was roused at 4 oclock in the morning and all hands went briskly to work getting ready to take the road early in order to keep ahead of Capt. Hedgepeth's company—but to our surprise a short time after sunrise one of our men sung out "there they come." Our men exerted themselves to the utmost to get into the road before this mammoth train came up, but to no purpose.

Before we were ready to take the road about 20 of Capt. H.'s wagons had passed & being mule teams were a little ahead of their friends who had ox teams, thereby leaving a vacancy between, which our company took advantage of, and drove in, making a continuous line of wagons for nearly a ¼ of a mile.

One of our wagons driven by Andrew B. Cole struck out on the grass for the purpose of passing the wagons in front and was followed by our whole train. After driving in this manner about 3 miles our train got ahead.

May 24th.
· While lying by this morning trains have been constantly passing. Today a train of government wagons 47 in number passed us and one Company of mounted men destined for the California service.

May 27th.
On the roadside today I saw a human scull with several names written upon it with pencil.

June 2nd.
We passed today a hunting party of the Sioux some 30 in number which we were not at all afraid of as their wives and children were along. About night we got down among the hollows & there not being grass enough in any one hollow for our stock we travelled on until 10 oclk at night when we reached the Platte bottom, but here the bottom was so narrow & so crowded with wagons as far as the eye could reach that we almost dispaired of finding camping place at all.

June 8th.
Passed over some rough road in the neighborhood of Scotts Bluffs [western Nebraska], passing the Black smiths shop about 35 miles below or east of Fort Laramie [in what is now Goshen County, Wyoming, on the left bank of the Laramie River, a short distance above its junction with the North Platte]. Here is some of the most beautiful scenery we have yet seen. Some of our party ascended the Bluff the next morning to get a view of the rocky mountains. When we arrived at the summit they were enveloped in dense fog and could see nothing.

June 16th.
Reached the lower platte Ferry about 10 oclk A.M. where we found some 2 or 300 wagons awaiting their turns to ferry. We understood that as many were assembled at the upper ferry [west of Casper, Wyoming].

June 18th.
Left the Platte for the last time and struck out across the most barren country we had ever yet seen. In addition to having little

71

or no grass our stock did not this day have a drop of water until sunset—all the water in this region being strongly impregnated with alkali and very poisonous. Passed a mineral spring but were afraid to use the water. We were overtaken this evening by the mormon mail & some of their party told us that by driving on to Willow Spring we would find excellent water & grass. We did so, making our drive some 32 miles & camping sometime after night. Find grass all eaten out. Stock fared badly.

June 20th.

Reached Independence Rock [central Wyoming] about 8 oclk this morning, a vast mass of bold barren rocks rising some hundred feet perpendicularly from the roads. Names innumerable we found here inscribed by travellers who had preceded us on this long tedious toilsome journey.

June 24th.

Reached the South Pass [Fremont County, Wyoming] & camped for the night, on the summit, where we found the grass superb. The assent to the summit of the Pass has been so gradual that we can scarcely realize that we have accomplished it.

July 2nd.

Reached Smith's fork of Bear River [near the western boundary of Wyoming] after a rough day's travel—where we found a large number of Snake Indians encamped. Here on account of the increased illness of Alfred Corum who had been sick a week or ten days we laid by a day.

July 3rd.

Whilst lying by some 200 wagons passed us & Alfred continued to grow worse & as there was no prospect of his living it

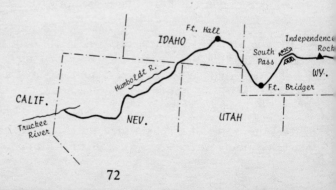

was deemed prudent for the wagons to start the next morning. Accordingly they left on the 4th leaving behind the Dearbourn [a four-wheeled carriage] & a party of 6 men to render every service to our dying friend. As there was no wood nor water near us we concluded to move him about 1½ miles where we found both. About 1 o'clock he died without a struggle and in full possession of all his faculties to the last.

July 23rd.
[At the Humboldt River, Nevada]

Drove 6 or 8 miles this morning & camped for the day as it was important to rest and graze our stock. Every other train is reduced to the same necessity. We learn that Capt. McCullocks ox train & Finley's banded together and destroyed the boat in which they ferried this stream in order to prevent the emigrants from following them.

July 25th.

A dusty barren bottom covered with the eternol dust from 6 to 8 inches deep.

Passed another grave today. These are melancholy sights to the travellor as they serve to remind him that he too may die far away from home & kindred, "a stranger in a strange land."

During the night the wolves were quite noisy & alarmed our mules.

July 26th.
[crossing the Humboldt Desert, Nevada]

Nothing but the sterile lands and dust immediately around us & naught in the distance to releave the eye, but bare rugged hills of basalt. Our feelings just now is that if we once get safely out of this great Basin we will not be cought here in a hurry.

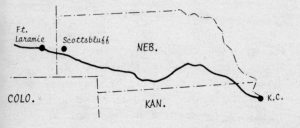

73

A continuance of yesterday's hard work & poor fare for our stock. We were struck with the contrast between our appearance now & when we left home. Then we had gay outriders prancing along proudly on their fiery steeds & our teams pressing forward with fierce resolution. Now what a scene—the teams crossing along slowly their gaunt sides marked with many a whip cut & their rigging defaced with dust—a sorry show. And where are all these gay outriders? Look before the train & you see them strung along the road for a mile on foot their faces and clothes covered with dust and looking worn & livid. What a picture.

July 30th.

We hear many reports hereabouts of the state of things in California. An express is said to have gone back to meet the troops destined for Oragon & turned them to California to repress the disorders of that Country.

Guerilla bands are said to be very troublesome—stopping wagons & pressing provisions as there is an absolute famine there at present. Gold they say is very abundant. We regret to hear these reports but if we knew them to be true & a return was practicable (which is not) we would still go on.

Men who have risked their lives by sickness, casualties, hardships of every kind and the remote prospect of starvation continually present to their minds are not to be detered from endeavoring to obtain some reward by the uncertain reports that float along this great highway.

They are now traversing the most difficult part of the route to California–the desert between the sink of the Humboldt River and the Truckee River, most of which lies within the present limits of Churchill County, Nevada, near Reno.

August 1st.

The mules were by this time so hungry that they greedily devoured the leaves of the willow. Fortunately we here found some grass—although of an inferior quality. This is a more trying time than any we have yet encountered & as we have yet some 71 miles to go over of the same kind of fare, we feel altogether uncertain about the result. We think, however, that at the worst we can walk the balance of the way.

August 4th.

A general panic now seezed upon all & doubt & fear prevailed every where. There is yet a stretch of 45 miles ahead of us without grass or water except at the boiling spring 25 miles from this point.

We left here at 4 oclk this evening & taking the right hand or old route travelled all night & reached the Hot Spring at daylight.

This is the most dreary desolate looking place we ever saw. It is on the top of a mountain & the water bubbles & boils up from the fissures in the rocks & forms into a small lake quite clear but so hot that it scalds. We dipped up the water & pourd it into some holes in the earth & cooled it & then watered our animals, mixed flour with it. The mules were so hungry that they ate dust & gravel & chewed up whatever came in their way—gearing, wagon covers or any thing they could reach.

August 5th.

We had 20 miles to accomplish & the heat of the day to make it. About 2 oclk we struck the heavy sand 10 miles from Truckey river & had the utmost difficulty in getting our stock thro—stopping every few yards to rest. A little before night we reached the [Truckee] river. We all felt greatly releaved. We found grass very abundant and the water very fine.

All along the desert road from the very start even the way side was strewed with the dead bodies of oxen, mules & horses & the stench was horrible. All our traveling experience furnishes no parallel for all this. Many persons suffered greatly for water during the last 8 or 10 miles, and many instances of noble generosity were developed on these occasions. Some trains that got over before us sent water back in kegs & left them on the road marked for the benefit of the feeble. We slept here for the first time for four nights.

THE PLAINS WERE BLACK WITH BUFFALO

The diary of John Bidwell's journey to California, printed in 1842, includes this description of vast herds of buffalo on the Western plains.

As soon as we struck the buffalo country we found a new source of interest. Before reaching the Platte we had seen an abundance of antelope and elk, prairie wolves and villages of prairie dogs, but only an occasional buffalo.

I think I can truly say that I saw in that region in one day more buffaloes than I have seen of cattle in all my life. I have seen the plain black with them for several days' journey as far as the eye could reach. They seemed to be coming northward continually from the distant plains to the Platte to get water, and would plunge in and swim across by thousands—so numerous were they that they changed not only the color of the water, but its taste, until it was unfit to drink; but we had to use it. One night when we were encamped on the South Fork of the Platte they came in such droves that we had to sit up and fire guns and make what fires we could to keep them from running over us and trampling us into the dust. We were obliged to go out some distance from camp to turn them: Captain Fitzpatrick told us that if we did not do this the buffaloes in front could not turn aside for the pressure of those behind. We could hear them thundering all night long; the ground fairly trembled with vast approaching bands; and if they had not been diverted, wagons, animals, and emigrants would have been trodden under their feet . . . .

THE PRAIRIE TRAVELER

One of the most popular travel guides of a century and more ago was a manual for westward-bound wagon trains and travelers, THE PRAIRIE TRAVELER, *first published in 1859. A travel guide for that purpose was not a description of the marvels to be seen along the way, but a collection of vital information needed for survival. A few samplings from this comprehensive work, reprinted here, suggest some of the knowledge needed for overland passage. It was written by Captain Randolph B. Marcy, one of the unsung explorers of the American West, at the request of the War Department. In the Civil War, Marcy served as Chief-of-Staff to his son-in-law, General George B. McClellan.*

After a particular route has been selected to make the journey across the plains, and the requisite number have arrived at the eastern terminus, their first business should be to organize themselves into a company and elect a commander. The company should be of sufficient magnitude to herd and guard animals, and for protection against Indians.

From 50 to 70 men, properly armed and equipped, will be enough for these purposes, and any greater number only makes the movements of the party more cumbersome and tardy.

In the selection of a captain, good judgment, integrity of purpose, and practical experience are the essential requisites, and these are indispensable to the harmony and consolidation of the association. His duty should be to direct the order of march, the time of starting and halting, to select the camps, detail and give orders to guards, and, indeed, to control and superintend all the movements of the company.

When a captain has once been chosen, he should be sustained in all his decisions unless he commit some manifest outrage, when a majority of the company can always remove him, and put a more competent man in his place. Sometimes men may be selected who, upon trial, do not come up to the anticipations of those who have placed them in power, and other men will exhibit, during the course of the march, more capacity. Under these circumstances it will not be unwise to make a change, the first election having been distinctly provisional.

WAGONS AND TEAMS.

Wagons should be of the simplest possible construction— strong, light, and made of well-seasoned timber, especially the wheels, as the atmosphere, in the elevated and arid region over which they have to pass, is so exceedingly dry during the summer months that, unless the wood-work is thoroughly seasoned, they will require constant repairs to prevent them from falling to pieces.

Spring wagons made in Concord, New Hampshire, are used to transport passengers and the mails upon some of the routes across the plains, and they are said, by those who have used them, to be much superior to any others. They are made of the close-grained oak that grows in a high northern latitude, and well seasoned.

There has been much discussion regarding the relative merits of mules and oxen for prairie traveling, and the question is yet far from being settled. Upon good firm roads, in a populated country, where grain can be procured, I should unquestionably give the preference to mules, as they travel faster, and endure the heat of summer much better than oxen; and if the journey be not over 1000 miles, and the grass abundant, even without grain, I think mules would be preferable. But when the march is to extend 1500 or 2000 miles, or over a rough sandy or muddy road, I believe young oxen will endure better than mules.

CLOTHING.

A suitable dress for prairie traveling is of great import to health and comfort. Cotton or linen fabrics do not sufficiently protect the body against the direct rays of the sun at midday, nor against rains or sudden changes of temperature. Wool, being a non-conductor, is the best material for this mode of locomotion, and should always be adopted for the plains. The coat should be short and stout, the shirt of red or blue flannel, such as can be found in almost all the shops on the frontier: this, in warm weather, answers for an outside garment. The pants should be of thick and soft woolen material, and it is well to have them re-enforced on the inside, where they come in contact with the saddle, with soft buckskin, which makes them more durable and comfortable.

Woolen socks and stout boots, coming up well at the knees, and made large, so as to admit the pants, will be found the best for horsemen, and they guard against rattlesnake bites.

The following list of articles is deemed a sufficient outfit for one man upon a three months' expedition, viz.:

2 blue or red flannel overshirts, open in front, with buttons.
2 woolen undershirts.
2 pairs thick cotton drawers.
4 pairs woolen socks.
2 pairs cotton socks.
4 colored silk handkerchiefs.
2 pairs stout shoes, for footmen.
1 pair boots, for horsemen.
1 pair shoes, for horsemen.
3 towels.
1 gutta percha poncho.
1 broad-brimmed hat of soft felt.

1 comb and brush.
2 tooth-brushes.
1 pound Castile soap.
3 pounds bar soap for washing clothes.
1 belt-knife and small whetstone.
Stout linen thread, large needles, a bit of beeswax, a few buttons, paper of pins, and a thimble, all contained in a small buckskin or stout cloth bag.

The foregoing articles, with the coat and overcoat, complete the wardrobe.

FUEL AND FIRE.

There are long distances upon some of the routes to California where no other fuel is found but the dried dung of the buffalo, called by the mountaineers "chips," and by the French "bois de vache," the *argul* of the Tartary deserts. It burns well when perfectly dry, answers a good purpose for cooking, and some men even prefer it to wood.

It is highly important that travelers should know the different methods that may be resorted to for kindling fires upon a march.

The most simple and most expeditious of these is by using the lucifer matches; but, unless they are kept in well-corked bottles, they are liable to become wet, and will then fail to ignite.

I have seen an Indian start a fire with flint and steel after others had failed to do it with matches. This was during a heavy rain, when almost all available fuel had become wet. On such occasions dry fuel may generally be obtained under logs, rocks, or leaning trees.

Should there be no other means of starting a fire, it can always be made with a gun or pistol, by placing upon the ground a rag saturated with damp powder, and a little dry powder sprinkled over it. The gun or pistol is then (uncharged) placed with the cone directly over and near the rag, and a cap exploded, which will invariably ignite it.

Inexperienced travelers are very liable, in kindling fires at their camp, to ignite the grass around them. Great caution should be taken to guard against the occurrence of such accidents, as they might prove exceedingly disastrous. We were very near having our entire train of wagons and supplies destroyed, upon one occasion, by the carelessness of one of our party in setting fire to the grass, and it was only by the most strenuous and well-timed efforts of two hundred men in setting counter fires, and burning around the train, that it was saved.

TRAILING.

I know of nothing in the woodman's education of so much importance, or so difficult to acquire, as the art of trailing or tracking men and animals. To become an adept in this art requires the constant practice of years, and with some men a lifetime does not suffice to learn it.

Almost all the Indians whom I have met with are proficient in this species of knowledge, the faculty for acquiring which appears to be innate with them. Exigencies of woodland and prairie-life stimulate the savage from childhood to develop faculties so important in the arts of war and of the chase.

A party of Indians, for example, starting out upon a war excursion, leave their families behind, and never transport their lodges; whereas, when they move with their families, they carry their lodges and other effects. If, therefore, an Indian trail is discovered with the marks of the lodge-poles upon it, it has certainly not been made by a war-party; but if the track do not

80

show the trace of lodge-poles, it will be equally certain that a war or hunting party has passed that way, and if it is not desired to come in conflict with them, their direction may be avoided.

It is not a difficult matter to distinguish the tracks of American horses from those of Indian horses, as the latter are never shod; moreover, they are much smaller.

MEETING INDIANS.

On approaching strangers these people put their horses at full speed, and persons not familiar with their peculiarities and habits might interpret this as an act of hostility; but it is their custom with friends as well as enemies, and should not occasion groundless alarm.

When a party is discovered approaching thus, and are near enough to distinguish signals, all that is necessary in order to ascertain their disposition is to raise the right hand with the palm in front, and gradually push it forward and back several times. They all understand this to be a command to halt, and if they are not hostile it will at once be obeyed.

After they have stopped the right hand is raised again as before, and slowly moved to the right and left, which signifies "I do not know you. Who are you?" As all the wild tribes have their peculiar pantomimic signals by which they are known, they will then answer the inquiry by giving their signal. If this should not be understood, they may be asked if they are friends by raising both hands grasped in the manner of shaking hands, or by locking the two fore-fingers firmly while the hands are held up. If friendly, they will respond with the same signal; but if enemies, they will probably disregard the command to halt, or give the signal of anger by closing the hand, placing it against the forehead, and turning it back and forth while in that position.

The pantomimic vocabulary is understood by all the Prairie Indians, and when oral communication is impracticable it constitutes the court or general council language of the Plains.

TELEGRAPHING BY SMOKES.

The transparency of the atmosphere upon the Plains is such that objects can be seen at great distances; a mountain, for example, presents a distinct and bold outline at fifty or sixty miles, and may occasionally be seen as far as a hundred miles.

The Indians, availing themselves of this fact, have been in the habit of practicing a system of telegraphing by means of smokes during the day and fires by night, and, I dare say, there are but few travelers who have crossed the mountains to California that have not seen these signals made and responded to from peak to peak in rapid succession.

Very dense smokes may be raised by kindling a large fire with dry wood, and piling upon it the green boughs of pine, balsam, or hemlock. This throws off a heavy cloud of black smoke which can be seen very far.

I shall not attempt at this time to present a matured system of signals, but will merely give a few suggestions tending to illustrate the advantages to be derived from the use of them.

For example, when two columns are marching through a country at such distances apart that smokes may be seen from one to the other, their respective positions may be made known to each other at any time by two smokes raised simultaneously or at certain preconcerted intervals.

Should the commander of one column desire to communicate with the other, he raises three smokes simultaneously, which, if seen by the other party, should be responded to in the same manner. They would then hold themselves in readiness for any other communications.

By multiplying the combinations of signals a great variety of messages might be transmitted in this manner; but, to avoid mistakes, the signals should be written down and copies furnished the commander of each separate party, and they need not necessarily be made known to other persons.

There is a certain relief in change, even though it be from bad to worse; as I have found in travelling in a stage-coach, that it is often a comfort to shift one's position and be bruised in a new place.

—Washington Irving

LINCOLN JOURNEYS TO WASHINGTON

On February 11, 1861, President-elect Abraham Lincoln left Springfield, Illinois, for his journey to the national capital. The trip was to take two weeks, instead of a possible two days, because he felt that personal appearances in a number of cities would help calm a nation shaken by secession and talk of war. The route of his train would wind through a half dozen states before terminating in Washington. Nothing untoward occurred during the wearisome trip until Philadelphia was reached on February 21, when he learned of a plot to assassinate him in Baltimore. Carl Sandburg describes the journey in ABRAHAM LINCOLN: THE PRAIRIE YEARS AND THE WAR YEARS.

He arrived in Philadelphia at four o'clock. In the hotel parlor Lincoln stood handshaking that night for an hour or two. Later in Norman B. Judd's room Lincoln met Allan Pinkerton, a railroad detective in the service of the Philadelphia, Wilmington & Baltimore Railroad, to guard trains and bridges and circumvent threatened explosions and fires. Pinkerton opened: "We have come to know, Mr. Lincoln, and beyond the shadow of a doubt, that there exists a plot to assassinate you. The attempt will be made on your way through Baltimore, day after tomorrow. I am here to help in outwitting the assassins." Lincoln sat with legs crossed, a good-natured curiosity on his face fading to a sober look. "I am listening, Mr. Pinkerton." A barber named Fernandina was foremost among the conspirators, according to Pinkerton's spies, who, he said, had been at work for weeks and had become "bosom friends and insepar-able companions" of the plotters. A melodramatic, maudlin speech by Fernandina at a secret meeting of the military com-pany he captained was described by Pinkerton to Lincoln, the barber waving "a long glittering knife" over his head and crying: "This hireling Lincoln shall never, never be President. My life is of no consequence in a cause like this, and I am willing to give it for his. As Orsini gave his life for Italy, I am ready to die for the rights of the South and to crush out the abolitionist."

Pinkerton went personally to Baltimore, purporting to be a Georgia secessionist, and "Fernandina cordially grasped my hand, and we all retired to a private saloon." Fernandina was asked if there was no other way to save the South than by killing Lincoln. He replied, in the Pinkerton report: "No, as well might you attempt to move the Washington Monument yonder with your breath, as to change our purpose. He must die—and die he shall." With another drink by this time, he was asked about the police. He had fixed that, too: "They are all with us. I have seen the Chief Marshal of Police, and he is all right. In a week from today, Lincoln will be a corpse." Also it seemed that Pinkerton detected another conspirator named Hill, who also drank heavy and often, and also was ready, in his talk, to kill Lincoln. He said, in the Pinkerton report, "I shall immortalize myself by plunging a knife into Lincoln's heart."

Lincoln interrupted with many questions. Supporting Pinker-ton's viewpoint were the practical Judd and the equally practi-cal Samuel M. Felton, a railroad president who considered the evidence positive of a plot to burn railroad bridges, blow up trains, "and murder Mr. Lincoln on his way to Washington." Pinkerton gave details of a wild-eyed plot. The police chief at Baltimore was arranging to send only a small force to the railroad depot, where a gang of toughs would start a fight to draw off the policemen. Then the Fernandina assassins would close round the President-elect and deliver the fatal shot or knife thrust. "We propose," said Pinkerton, "to take you on to Washington this very night, Mr. President, and steal a march on your enemies."

Lincoln deliberated, then: "Gentlemen, I appreciate the suggestions, and while I can stand anything essential in the way of misrepresentation, I do not feel I can go to Washington tonight. Tomorrow morning I have promised to raise the flag over Independence Hall, and after that to visit the legislature at Harrisburg. Whatever the cost, these two promises I must fulfill. Thereafter I shall be ready to consider any plan you may adopt."

From Washington that night arrived Frederick W. Seward, son of Lincoln's announced Secretary of State. He found Chestnut Street and the Continental Hotel gay with a serenade to the President-elect, music, flowers, flags, buzzing conversations, and "brilliantly lighted parlours filled with ladies and gentlemen who had come to 'pay their respects.' " Lamon took Seward to Lincoln's bedroom. "Presently Colonel Lamon called me," wrote Seward of that night, "and we met Mr. Lincoln coming down the hall . . . After friendly greeting he sat down by the table under the gas light to peruse the letter I had brought." The communications his father had so secretly and hurriedly sent on, which Lincoln read deliberately twice, stressed a report of one Colonel Stone:

> A New York detective officer on duty in Baltimore for three weeks past reports this morning that there is serious danger of violence to, and the assassination of, Mr. Lincoln in his passage through that city, should the time of that passage be known. He states that there are banded rowdies holding secret meetings, and that he has heard threats of mobbing and violence, and has himself heard men declare that if Mr. Lincoln was to be assassinated they would like to be the men. . . All risk might be easily avoided by a change in the traveling arrangements which would bring Mr. Lincoln and a portion of his party through Baltimore by a night train without previous notice.

"Did you hear any names mentioned?" Lincoln pressed. "Did you, for instance, ever hear anything said about such a name as Pinkerton?" No, Seward had heard no such name. Lincoln smiled. "If different persons, not knowing of each other's work, have been pursuing separate clues that led to the same result, why then it shows there may be something in it. But if this is only the same story, filtered through two channels, and reaching me in two ways, then that don't make it any stronger. Don't you see?" They discussed it further and Lincoln rose, "Well, we haven't got to decide it tonight, anyway."

In studying what to do Lincoln had to consider the silence of

Baltimore and Maryland. Governor Thomas H. Hicks of that state favored the Union as against secession and was himself threatened with death by men proclaiming their volunteer militia would shoot down Northern soldiers en route to Washington, would burn supply depots and railroad bridges, would if war came march their corps to Washington and take that city. Governor Hicks had a seething and sensitive public to handle, a people ready to show what they could do with guns, clubs, stones, bricks, in street fighting. The marshal of police, George P. Kane, was an open secessionist.

At six o'clock that morning of February 22, Washington's Birthday, Lincoln amid cannon salutes and crowd applause pulled a rope and raised a flag over Independence Hall. Inside Independence Hall he spoke to an audience crowding all corners and overflowing. He had often pondered over the "dangers" incurred by the men who has assembled there and framed the Declaration. Not merely separation from a motherland, but liberty as a hope to all the world, for all future time, was the sentiment guiding them. "It was that which gave promise that in due time the weights should be lifted from the shoulders of all men, and that all should have an equal chance . . ." He asked if the country could be saved on that basis. If so he would consider himself one of the happiest men in the world. "But, if this country cannot be saved without giving up that principle—I was about to say I would rather be assassinated on this spot than surrender it." He could see no need of bloodshed and war. "And I may say in advance, there will be no blood shed unless it be forced upon the Government . . ."

Judd had been up nearly the whole night in a conference with Pinkerton and other men. They arranged for Lincoln to journey from Harrisburg on a two-car train that night under conditions they believed would deliver him safely in Washington the next morning. In Harrisburg, amid guns and platoons, Lincoln replied to Governor Curtin's welcome that under the weight of his great responsibility he brought an honest heart, but "I dare not tell you that I bring a head sufficient for it." He would lean on the people. "If my own strength should fail, I shall at least fall back upon these masses, who, I think, under any circumstances will not fail."

That evening Lincoln was at a table in the dining room of the

86

Jones House in Harrisburg. He had made three speeches during the day, listened to other speeches longer than his own, talked with Governor Curtin and men of power in Pennsylvania, and held a conference with members of his party. For the first time others than Judd learned of the change in plans. Judd had told Lincoln these other old friends should know what was afoot, Lincoln approving. "I reckon they will laugh at us, Judd, but you had better get them together."

Lincoln told them, "Unless there are some other reasons besides fear of ridicule, I am disposed to carry out Judd's plan." A. K. McClure, legislative member and a founder of the Republican party, was sure he heard Lincoln say, "What would the nation think of its President stealing into its capital like a thief in the night?" while Governor Curtin declared the question not one for Lincoln to decide.

Close to six o'clock Lincoln was called from the dinner table, went upstairs to his room, changed his dinner dress for a traveling suit, and came down with a soft felt hat sticking in his pocket, and a folded shawl on his arm. A carriage was ready. Then, as Judd told it: "Mr. Lamon went first into the carriage; Col. Sumner of the regular army, was following close after Mr. Lincoln; I put my hand gently on his shoulder; he turned to see what was wanted, and before I could explain the carriage was off. The situation was a little awkward." Judd had tricked Colonel Sumner into a moment of delay, and to the Colonel's furious words Judd replied, "When we get to Washington, Mr. Lincoln shall determine what apology is due you."

Lincoln and Lamon, with a lone car to themselves, drawn by a lone locomotive of the Pennsylvania Railroad, rode out of Harrisburg, no lights on, Lamon carrying two ordinary pistols, two derringers and two large knives. Telegraph linemen had cut the wires; all telegrams into or out of Harrisburg were shut off till further orders.

In Philadephia shortly after ten a carriage with Detective Pinkerton and Superintendent Kenney of the P. W. & B. Railroad met Lincoln and Lamon at the Pennsylvania Railroad station and took them to the P. W. & B. station, where they were put on the last car of the New York-Washington train. A woman detective working for Pinkerton had reserved rear berths of a sleeping-car, one for her "invalid brother" to be occupied by

Lincoln, who was quickly in his berth with the curtains carefully drawn.

Unknown to Pinkerton or Lamon, on that last car a powerfully built man, armed with a revolver, slept in a berth engaged at New York. He was Superintendent John A. Kennedy of the New York police department, an officer of valor and integrity, who did not know that his detective, Bookstaver, had rushed on to Washington and reported his Baltimore findings to Seward. Kennedy was acting on reports received from his other two men in Baltimore, and his intention, as he slept in the same car with Lincoln that night, was to warn the authorities in Washington next morning that Lincoln would require safeguarding in his scheduled trip across Maryland the next day.

Baltimore was reached at 3:30 in the morning, and of the stop there Pinkerton wrote: "An officer of the road entered the car and whispered in my ear the welcome words 'All's well' . . ." An hour and more the train waited for a connecting train from the west. A drunken traveler on the train platform sang "Dixie," sang over and again how he would live and die in dear old Dixie. Lincoln murmured sleepily, said Pinkerton, "No doubt there will be a great time in Dixie by and by." Except for "a joke or two in an undertone," Lincoln was not heard from during the night, according to Lamon. At six in the morning the President-elect stepped off the train in Washington.

Been flying, train-riding, automobiling, horseback and buggy riding over Texas for thirty-three years and I've never seen a tenth of it. If it had been in Europe, eighty wars would have been fought over it. There is single ranches here bigger than France. Counties bigger than England. Saddle Horse pastures big as Alsace-Lorraine. The lakes of Switzerland would be buffalo wallows in Texas. It's located between Mexico and the United States to keep Mexico from annexing the United States . . .

—Will Rogers

88

AN EARLY PIGGY-BACK

An Englishman traveling by railroad from Philadelphia to Baltimore in 1861 found the arrangements for crossing the Susquehanna River ingenious but casual. An excerpt from Anthony Trollope's NORTH AMERICA.

The railway from Philadelphia to Baltimore passes along the top of Chesapeake Bay and across the Susquehanna River; at least the railway cars do. On one side of the river they are run on to a huge ferryboat, and are again run off at the other side. Such an operation would seem to be one of difficulty to us under any circumstances; but as the Susquehanna is a tidal river, rising and falling a considerable number of feet, the natural impediment in the way of such an enterprise would, I think, have staggered us. We should have built a bridge costing two or three millions sterling, on which no conceivable amount of traffic would pay a fair dividend. Here, in crossing the Susquehanna, the boat is so constructed that its deck shall be level with the line of the railway at half tide, so that the inclined plane from the shore down to the boat, or from the shore up to the boat, shall never exceed half the amount of the rise or fall. One would suppose that the most intricate machinery would have been necessary for such an arrangement; but it was all rough and simple, and apparently managed by two negroes ... The cars were dragged up the inclined plane by a hawser attached to an engine, which hawser, had the stress broken it, as I could not but fancy probable, would have flown back and cut to pieces a lot of us who were standing in front of the car. But I do not think that any such accident would have caused very much attention. Life and limbs are not held to be so precious here as they are in England.

Anthony Trollope was also astounded by the imperturbability of the passengers under trying circumstances.

In running down the mountains to Pittsburgh an accident occurred which in any other country would have thrown the engine off the line and reduced the carriages behind the engine to a heap of ruins. But here it had no other effect than that of delaying us for three or four hours. The tire of one of the heavy driving wheels flew off, and in the shock the body of the wheel itself was broken, one spoke and a portion of the circumference of the wheel was carried away, and the steam-chamber ripped open. Nevertheless the train was pulled up, neither the engine nor any of the carriages got off the line, and the men in charge of the train seemed to think very lightly of the matter. I was amused to see how little of the affair was made by any of the passengers. In England a delay of three hours would in itself produce a great amount of grumbling, or at least many signs of discomfort and temporary unhappiness. But here no one said a word. Some of the younger men got out and looked at the ruined wheel; but most of the passengers kept their seats, chewed their tobacco, and went to sleep.

THE RAILWAY TRAIN

I like to see it lap the miles,
And lick the valleys up,
And stop to feed itself at tanks;
And then, prodigious, step

Around a pile of mountains,
And, supercilious, peer
In shanties by the side of roads;
And then a quarry pare

To fit its sides, and crawl between,
Complaining all the while
In horrid, hooting stanza;
Then chase itself down hill

And neigh like Boanerges;
Then, punctual as a star,
Stop—docile and omnipotent—
At its own stable door.

—Emily Dickinson

A STAGECOACH JOURNEY

His career as a Mississippi River pilot ended by the outbreak of the Civil War, Missouri-born Samuel L. Clemens served for a few weeks as a Confederate "irregular." Then, feeling he was not built for soldiering, he decided to take Horace Greeley's advice and go West. The trip was made in company with his older brother Orion, a Unionist, who had been appointed Secretary of the Territory of Nevada and had suggested that 26-year-old Sam go along with him as his secretary, unpaid. They left St. Joseph, Missouri, then considered the edge of civilization, in July of 1861. The younger brother's accompanying hilarious account of their journey across the plains by stagecoach is extracted from the opening chapters of ROUGHING IT, *written in 1871 after Clemens had gained considerable fame as an author and lecturer using the nom de plume Mark Twain.*

The first thing we did on that glad evening that landed us at St. Joseph was to hunt up the stage office, and pay a hundred and fifty dollars apiece for tickets per overland coach to Carson City, Nevada.

The next morning, bright and early, we took a hasty breakfast and hurried to the starting place. Then an inconvenience presented itself which we had not properly appreciated before, namely, that one cannot make a heavy traveling trunk stand for twenty-five pounds of baggage—because it weighs a good deal more. But that was all we could take—twenty-five pounds each. So we had to snatch our trunks open and make a selection in a good deal of a hurry. We put our lawful twenty-five pounds apiece all in one valise, and shipped the trunks back to St. Louis again. It was a sad parting, for now we had no swallow-tail coats and white kid gloves to wear at Pawnee receptions in the Rocky

Mountains, and no stovepipe hats nor patent-leather boots, nor anything else necessary to make life calm and peaceful. We were reduced to a war footing. Each of us put on a rough, heavy suit of clothing, woolen army shirt and "stogy" boots included; and into the valise we crowded a few white shirts, some underclothing, and such things. My brother, the Secretary, took along about four pounds of United States statutes and six pounds of unabridged dictionary; for we did not know—poor innocents—that such things could be bought in San Francisco on one day and received in Carson City the next. I was armed to the teeth with a pitiful little Smith & Wesson's seven-shooter, which carried a ball like a homeopathic pill, and it took the whole seven to make a dose for an adult. But I thought it was grand. It appeared to me to be a dangerous weapon. It only had one fault—you could not hit anything with it. One of our "conductors" practiced awhile on a cow with it, and as long as she stood still and behaved herself she was safe; but as soon as she went to moving about, and he got to shooting at other things, she came to grief. The Secretary had a small-sized Colt's revolver strapped around him for protection against the Indians, and to guard against accidents he carried it uncapped. Mr. George Bemis was dismally formidable. George Bemis was our fellow traveler. We had never seen him before. He wore in his belt an old original "Allen" revolver, such as irreverent people called a "pepperbox." Simply drawing the trigger back, cocked and fired the pistol. As the trigger came back, the hammer would begin to rise and the barrel to turn over, and presently down would drop the hammer, and away would speed the ball. To aim along the turning barrel and hit the thing aimed at was a feat which was probably never done with an "Allen" in the world. But George's was a reliable weapon, nevertheless, because, as one of the stage drivers afterward said, "If she didn't get what she went after, she would fetch something else." And so she did. She went after a deuce of spades nailed against a tree, once, and fetched a mule standing about thirty yards to the left of it. Bemis did not want the mule; but the owner came out with a double-barreled shotgun and persuaded him to buy it anyhow. It was a cheerful weapon—the "Allen." Sometimes all its six barrels would go off at once, and then there was no safe place in all the region roundabout but behind it.

We took two or three blankets for protection against frosty weather in the mountains. In the matter of luxuries we were modest—we took none along but some pipes and five pounds of smoking tobacco. We had two large canteens to carry water in, between stations on the plains, and we also took with us a little shot bag of silver coin for daily expenses in the way of breakfasts and dinners.

By eight o'clock everything was ready, and we were on the other side of the river. We jumped into the stage, the driver cracked his whip, and we bowled away and left "the States" behind us. It was a superb summer morning, and all the landscape was brilliant with sunshine. There was a freshness and breeziness, too, and an exhilarating sense of emancipation from all sorts of cares and responsibilities, that almost made us feel that the years we had spent in the close, hot city, toiling and slaving, had been wasted and thrown away. We were spinning along through Kansas, and in the course of an hour and a half we were fairly abroad on the great plains. Just here the land was rolling—a grand sweep of regular elevations and depressions as far as the eye could reach—like the stately heave and swell of the ocean's bosom after a storm. And everywhere were cornfields, accenting with squares of deeper green this limitless expanse of grassy land. But presently this sea upon dry ground was to lose its "rolling" character and stretch away for seven hundred miles as level as a floor!

Our coach was a great swinging and swaying stage, of the most sumptuous description—an imposing cradle on wheels. It was drawn by six handsome horses, and by the side of the driver sat the "conductor," the legitimate captain of the craft; for it was his business to take charge and care of the mails, baggage, express matter, and passengers. We three were the only passengers this trip. We sat on the back seat, inside. About all the rest of the coach was full of mailbags—for we had three days' delayed mails with us. Almost touching our knees, a perpendicular wall of mail matter rose up to the roof. There was a great pile of it strapped on top of the stage, and both the fore and hind boots were full. We had twenty-seven hundred pounds of it aboard, the driver said—"a little for Brigham, and Carson, and 'Frisco, but the heft of it for the Injuns, which is powerful troublesome 'thout they get plenty of truck to read." But as he

93

just then got up a fearful convulsion of his countenance which was suggestive of a wink being swallowed by an earthquake, we guessed that his remark was intended to be facetious, and to mean that we would unload the most of our mail matter somewhere on the plains and leave it to the Indians, or whosoever wanted it.

We changed horses every ten miles, all day long, and fairly flew over the hard, level road. We jumped out and stretched our legs every time the coach stopped, and so the night found us still vivacious and unfatigued.

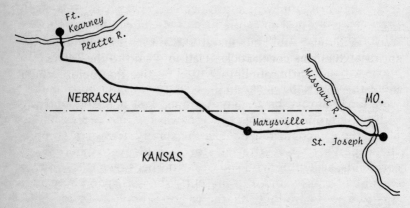

About an hour and a half before daylight we were bowling along smoothly over the road—so smoothly that our cradle only rocked in a gently, lulling way, that was gradually soothing us to sleep, and dulling our consciousness—when something gave away under us! We were dimly aware of it, but indifferent to it. The coach stopped. We heard the driver and conductor talking together outside, and rummaging for a lantern, and swearing because they could not find it—but we had no interest in whatever had happened, and it only added to our comfort to think of those people out there at work in the murky night, and we snug in our nest with the curtains drawn. But presently, by the sounds, there seemed to be an examination going on, and then the driver's voice said:

"By George, the thoroughbrace is broke!"

This startled me broad awake—as an undefined sense of calamity is always apt to do. I said to myself: "Now, a thoroughbrace is probably part of a horse; and doubtless a vital part, too, from the dismay in the driver's voice. Leg, maybe— and yet how could he break his leg waltzing along such a road as this? No, it can't be his leg. That is impossible, unless he was reaching for the driver. Now, what can be the thoroughbrace of a horse, I wonder? Well, whatever comes, I shall not air my ignorance in this crowd, anyway."

Just then the conductor's face appeared at a lifted curtain, and his lantern glared in on us and our wall of mail matter. He said:

"Gents, you'll have to turn out a spell. Thoroughbrace is broke."

We climbed out into a chill drizzle, and felt ever so homeless and dreary. When I found that the thing they called a "thoroughbrace" was the massive combination of belts and springs which the coach rocks itself in, I said to the driver:

"I never saw a thoroughbrace used up like that before, that I can remember. How did it happen?"

"Why, it happened by trying to make one coach carry three days' mail—that's how it happened," said he. "And right here is the very direction which is wrote on all the newspaper bags which was to be put out for the Injuns for to keep 'em quiet. It's most uncommon lucky, becuz it's so nation dark I should 'a' gone by unbeknowns if that air thoroughbrace hadn't broke."

I knew that he was in labor with another of those winks of his, though I could not see his face, because he was bent down at work; and wishing him a safe delivery, I turned to and helped the rest get out the mail sacks. It made a great pyramid by the roadside when it was all out. When they had mended the thoroughbrace we filled the two boots again, but put no mail on top, and only half as much inside as there was before. The conductor bent all the seat backs down, and then filled the coach just half full of mailbags from end to end. We objected loudly to this, for it left us no seats. But the conductor was wiser than we, and said a bed was better than seats, and moreover, this plan would protect his thoroughbraces. We never wanted any seats after that. The lazy bed was infinitely preferable. I had many an exciting day, subsequently, lying on it reading the statutes and the dictionary, and wondering how the characters would turn out.

The conductor said he would send back a guard from the next

station to take charge of the abandoned mailbags, and we drove on.

It was now just dawn; and as we stretched our cramped legs full length on the mail sacks, and gazed out through the windows across the wide wastes of greensward clad in cool, powdery mist, to where there was an expectant look in the eastern horizon, our perfect enjoyment took the form of a tranquil and contented ecstasy. The stage whirled along at a spanking gait, the breeze flapping curtains and suspended coats in a most exhilarating way; the cradle swayed and swung luxuriously; the pattering of the horses' hoofs, the cracking of the driver's whip, and his "Hi-yi! g'lang!" were music; the spinning ground and the waltzing trees appeared to give us a mute hurrah as we went by, and then slack up and look after us with interest, or envy, or something; and as we lay and smoked the pipe of peace and compared all this luxury with the years of tiresome city life that had gone before it, we felt that there was only one complete and satisfying happiness in the world, and we had found it.

After breakfast, at some station whose name I have forgotten, we three climbed up on the seat behind the driver, and let the conductor have our bed for a nap. And by and by, when the sun made me drowsy, I lay down on my face on top of the coach, grasping the slender iron railing, and slept for an hour or more. That will give one an appreciable idea of those matchless roads. Instinct will make a sleeping man grip a fast hold of the railing when the stage jolts, but when it only swings and sways, no grip is necessary. Overland drivers and conductors used to sit in their places and sleep thirty or forty minutes at a time, on good roads, while spinning along at the rate of eight or ten miles an hour. I saw them do it, often. There was no danger about it; a sleeping man will seize the irons in time when the coach jolts. These men were hard worked, and it was not possible for them to stay awake all the time.

By and by we passed through Marysville, and over the Big Blue and Little Sandy; thence about a mile, and entered Nebraska. About a mile further on, we came to the Big Sandy—one hundred and eighty miles from St. Joseph.

As the sun went down and the evening chill came on, we made preparation for bed. We stirred up the hard leather letter sacks, and the knotty canvas bags of printed matter (knotty and uneven because of projecting ends and corners of magazines, boxes, and books). We stirred them up and redisposed them in such a way as to make our bed as level as possible. And we did improve it, too, though after all our work it had an upheaved and billowy look about it, like a little piece of a stormy sea. Next we hunted up our boots from odd nooks among the mailbags where they had settled, and put them on. Then we got down our coats, vests, pantaloons, and heavy woolen shirts from the arm loops where they had been swinging all day, and clothed ourselves in them—for, there being no ladies either at the stations or in the coach, and the weather being hot, we had looked to our comfort by stripping to our underclothing, at nine o'clock in the morning. All things being now ready, we stowed the uneasy dictionary where it would lie as quiet as possible, and placed the water canteens and pistols where we could find them in the dark. Then we smoked a final pipe, and swapped a final yarn; after which, we put the pipes, tobacco, and bag of coin in snug holes and caves among the mailbags, and then fastened down the coach curtains all around, and made the place as "dark as the inside of a cow," as the conductor phrased it in his picturesque way. It was certainly as dark as any place could be— nothing was even dimly visible in it. And finally, we rolled ourselves up like silkworms, each person in his own blanket, and sank peacefully to sleep.

Whenever the stage stopped to change horses, we would wake up, and try to recollect where we were—and succeed—and in a minute or two the stage would be off again, and we likewise. We began to get into country, now, threaded here and there with little streams. These had high, steep banks on each side, and every time we flew down one bank and scrambled up the other, our party inside got mixed somewhat. First we would all be down in a pile at the forward end of the stage, nearly in a sitting posture, and in a second we would shoot to the other end, and stand on our heads. And we would sprawl and kick, too, and ward off ends and corners of mailbags that came lumbering over us and about us; and as the dust rose from the tumult, we would all sneeze in chorus, and the majority of us would grumble, and probably say some hasty thing, like: "Take your elbow out of my ribs! Can't you quit crowding?"

Every time we avalanched from one end of the stage to the

other, the unabridged dictionary would come too; and every time it came it damaged somebody. One trip it "barked" the secretary's elbow; the next trip it hurt me in the stomach, and the third it tilted Bemis's nose up till he could look down his nostrils—he said. The pistols and coin soon settled to the bottom, but the pipes, pipe stems, tobacco, and canteens clattered and floundered after the dictionary every time it made an assault on us, and aided and abetted the book by spilling tobacco in our eyes, and water down our backs.

Still, all things considered, it was a very comfortable night. It wore gradually away, and when at last a cold gray light was visible through the puckers and chinks in the curtains, we yawned and stretched with satisfaction, shed our cocoons, and felt that we had slept as much as was necessary. By and by, as the sun rose up and warmed the world, we pulled off our clothes and got ready for breakfast. We were just pleasantly in time, for five minutes afterward the driver sent the weird music of his bugle winding over the grassy solitudes, and presently we detected a low hut or two in the distance. Then the rattling of the coach, the clatter of our six horses' hoofs, and the driver's crisp commands awoke to a louder and stronger emphasis, and we went sweeping down on the station at our smartest speed. It was fascinating—that old overland stagecoaching.

Even as late as 1870 many roads . . . were only clearings through forest, with few level stretches and often with stumps left in the middle of the road. In that year the Governor of Connecticut wrote, "What we complain of under the present condition of affairs is that all four wheels of our wagons are often running on different grades. This kind of road will throw a child out of its mother's arms. We let our road-makers shake us enough to the mile to furnish assault and battery cases for a thousand police cases."

—From *Our Vanishing Landscape*, by Eric Sloane

BY DOG SLED TO THE YUKON RIVER

At the close of the Civil War the Western Union Telegraph Company, impatient with Cyrus Field's unsuccessful attempts to lay an Atlantic cable, decided to try joining Europe and America with a telegraph line running from San Francisco up the West Coast to Bering Strait, then down the coast of Asia to connect with a line being pushed across Siberia by the Russians. Accompanying one of the construction crews to Alaska (then called Russian America) was Frederick Whymper, a youthful English adventurer, writer, and artist. Whymper seems not to have been overburdened with work for Western Union. In his lavishly-illustrated book TRAVEL AND ADVENTURE IN THE TERRITORY OF ALASKA *(published in 1868, reissued facsimile in 1968 by University Microfilms, Ann Arbor, Michigan) he describes a 170-mile journey by dog sled from Unalachleet, a Russian trading post on Norton Sound, to Nulato, another on the great Yukon River, a prelude to a 600-mile trip up the river in a sealskin boat to the Hudson's Bay Company post at Fort Yukon. The following account is condensed from Whymper's diary of the sled trip, which began October 27, 1866, just four months before Secretary of State William H. Seward surprised the world by purchasing Alaska from Russia for the paltry sum of $7,200,000.*

Although our expedition was well fitted out in the absolute essentials of travel, no provision had been made with regard to either sledges or dogs, it having been very naturally supposed that the country itself was the best source from whence to obtain these. We found, however, that the dogs were neither plentiful nor of a good class. They were hardly above the average of the sneaking, snarling Indian curs of Oregon and British Columbia, and it was very difficult to make them attached to you,—a proof to my mind that they had as much of the wolf as the dog in them. They are very hairy, are of all colours, iron grey predominating, have wolfish features and short legs, but their immense bushy tails make up for all deficiencies. Taking them all in all, they did good service in transporting our goods.

On the morning of the 27th October, at eleven o'clock, we bade adieu to our friends, some of whom persisted in accompanying us a little way on the frozen surface of the Unalachleet River, whilst the others honoured us with a grand, but rather irregular volley of blank-cartridge from revolvers, muskets, and the old battered cannon of the Russian post. Our party comprised nine persons, as follows:—Captain Ketchum and Lieutenant Labarge, his right-hand man, Mr. Dall, a collector for the Smithsonian Institute, myself, and Pickett, a man detailed for our service. Mr. Francis, engineer of our little steamer, and three Indians completed our list. We took four sledges, each drawn by five dogs, and very well laden with a miscellaneous collection of boxes, barrels, tools, furs, blankets, and snow shoes.

The day was beautifully calm and clear, the temperature just before starting was $+5°$ Fahr., but got much colder during the day. As we had to run alongside of, or behind our sledges, we soon found that the heavy fur clothing, so very comfortable when stationary, was infinitely too much for us when in violent exercise, and we accordingly divested ourselves of much of it. We found the frozen river, on whose surface we travelled all day, for the most part well covered with snow.

A few small accidents varied the day's travel, such as the bone runners of our sledges cracking off, or the dogs getting loose and making a break for the woods. At four o'clock in the afternoon we stopped for a rest, raised a good fire of driftwood on the surface of the ice, and then cooked our bacon and made some refreshing tea. We then resumed our trip by starlight, hoping to make the Indian village of Igtigalik the same evening. About six o'clock we came to a standstill; a great patch of the river was entirely open, nor could we see a way round. Attempting to creep round the shelving banks our sledges were half-buried in the soft snow, and as the night was very dark, and we did not wish to risk losing our loads in the river, we came to the conclusion that we must camp.

We had unfortunately relied on the next village for a supply of dog-feed. The Russian post we had just left was famous for "ukalee," an inferior kind of salmon dried for this purpose; but our men wintering there would, we knew, require so much of it that we had determined to obtain ours on the route. Our sledges, too, were otherwise filled to their uttermost capacity. The poor dogs passed a hungry night, howling dismally. We had to place everything eatable out of their reach, and as they did not object to skin clothing or old boots, and would readily devour their own harness, it was a somewhat difficult task.

The morning of the 28th we found that four of our dogs, disgusted and hungry, had deserted from our service, and we were sure that they had "made tracks" for the Russian post. We made an early start in the brisk cold morning (temp. −6° Fahr.), and reached the village without any trouble, after we had passed round the edge of the open water just mentioned. There, however, the thin ice cracked beneath the weight of our sledges, and we "kept moving," expecting a ducking every moment.

On the right bank of the river we found a number of Indian summer dwellings,—simply wooden shanties, built above ground, with a small doorway, sometimes circular, and a hole in the roof to let out the smoke.

On the left bank were a few underground houses, intended for winter use. These were simply square holes in the ground, roofed in, and earthed over. The entrance of each was always a rude shanty of logs or planks, passing into which we found a hole in the ground, the entrance to a subterranean passage. Into this we dropped, and crawled on our hands and knees into the room. "Amilka," the owner of one of these houses, put half his floor at our disposal, and we cleared it of dirt and encumbrances, and spread our skins over it. A part of us stopped there some days, studying the manners and customs of the people.

During our stay at the village, on October 30th and 31st, and on the 1st November, a thaw set in; the thermometer standing at points between +32° and +35° Fahr., and the wind south. Snow also fell. On the 2nd, Dall and Francis returned to Unalachleet, with the hope of recovering our dogs, several more of whom had left our service.

On the 3rd we started with four sledges for the upper village of Ulukuk, a distance of fifteen miles. Our route lay mainly on a "peronose" (as the Russians term a portage), over land thickly covered with soft snow, in which our dogs, sledges, and selves were half buried. On the top of an ordinary sledge load we carried our skin canoe, and had no small work in helping it along, more especially at snow banks. We crossed many small streams, on which the ice was not thoroughly formed, slipping into rather cool water up to our waists. We carefully lifted our sledges over such places to prevent wetting our goods. On some of the tributaries of the river the route was like a well-made road, with but a slight covering of snow, and we occasionally got a few minutes' ride. It was, however, a luxury but rarely attained. In the woods, through which our course partly lay, the dogs invariably ran the sledges against the trees and stumps, and there they would remain, till two or three of us could clear them. Late in the day we arrived at the Ulukuk River, which was still open. Rapids abound in it; and there are warm springs in the neighbourhood, so that this stream is but rarely quite frozen up.

Ulukuk is the paradise of this part of the country in regard to salmon, salmon-trout, grouse, and deer meat; and a larger number of Ingeletes congregate there than in any other of their villages. There is no fear of your dogs deserting from such a place.

The common native mode of cooking is roasting by the fire; some of them have, however, bought iron pots from the Russians. Salmon cooked on a stick placed near the fire, and occasionally turned till "done brown," is luscious.

On the 4th a terrible snow-storm occurred, with a strong N.E. wind. We were fortunately at that time in an underground house, exhibiting our treasures in magnetic compasses, pencils, note-books, &c., to an admiring crowd, and trading with them for dried fish for our dogs.

On the morning of the 5th we turned our skin canoe to good

account by using it to cross the Ulukuk River. By making several trips, we transported to the opposite bank our sledges, dogs, and goods. At Ulukuk I essayed my first pair of snow shoes, to the amusement of the natives, who wondered where a man could have been all his life who had not become familiar with their use!

On the 6th we made a start, taking two sledges, an Indian man, and a boy; the latter we named "Tommy." We "cached" our skin-boat; it was to be brought up for us at a later period. The day was pleasant—temperature +23° Fahr.;—but the snow was fresh and soft, and all of our party wore snow shoes. After a little use, I became quite proficient. The only secret in wearing them is to strive to forget you have them on at all, and to walk exactly as you would anywhere else. The snow shoe then moves forward with the foot, but is not lifted much above the snow, and the lashings are so arranged that the toe remains fixed, while the rest of the foot moves up and down in the usual manner. Of course, the great object in using them is to diffuse your whole weight over a large surface, and they are usually of a good length, sometimes five and a-half feet long and upwards. An average length is four and a-half feet. All used in this part of the country are rounded and bent upwards in front, and pointed behind. They are made of birch-wood, covered at either end with a fine network of gut; the lashings for the foot are strips of hide.

At 4 we reached the base of the "Versola Sofka" Mountain, where we found a large frozen stream. We camped hard by it, and made a glorious fire and a bed of aromatic fir-brush; a screen of canvas, fixed behind our camp to the trees, and our snow shoes stuck in the ground, sheltered us from the only enemy we feared—the wind. We found from experience that tents were not in winter as comfortable as these open camps, as they could not be with safety placed sufficiently near the fire. After having arranged the camp, unloaded the sledges as far as necessary, and fed our dogs, we divested ourselves of our damp fur socks and skin boots, and hung them up to dry at a moderate distance from the fire. Our Indian meantime took the pots, and went to break a hole in the nearest frozen stream, to get the water for our tea. One of us sliced the bacon, got out a bag of "hard bread," or biscuit, or set to work concocting a stew of dried deer-meat or fresh grouse. Soon our meal was over, the ever grateful pipe smoked by one and all of us, and we turned into our blankets and furs, and in a few minutes we were soundly sleeping. We woke in the morning to find our breath congealed in masses of ice on our moustachios and other hairy appendages.

We left the "Versola Sofka" on the morning of the 7th, and, finding the loads too great for our dogs under the circumstances, we raised an erection of poles, and deposited some bags thereon. I may here say, once for all, that our men often left goods, consisting of tea, flour, molasses, bacon, and all kinds of miscellaneous items—scattered in this way over the country, and that they remained untouched by the Indians, who frequently travelled past them. It would require some faith in one's species to do the same in St. James's Park!

On the 8th snow fell thickly, and travelling was so difficult that with our best exertions we did not make ten miles during the day. We camped thoroughly worn out. Although the use of snow shoes renders travelling possible, where otherwise it would hardly be so, they are very fatiguing in soft or soggy snow.

The morning of the 9th broke fine and clear, with a temperature of +4° Fahr., and we travelled with greater ease through level country diversified by low rises from which we could see the break in the hills towards the Yukon. Our Indian, proceeding a good way a-head, shot several ptarmigan, and we made a fair day's journey of eighteen miles before camping, The next morning a north wind blew, and made us feel the cold very decidedly. It is wonderful how searching the wind is in this Arctic climate: each little seam, slit, or tear in your fur or woollen clothing makes you aware of its existence; and one's nose, ears, and angles generally, are specially the sufferers. We passed this day over a rather more hilly country (in a north-east direction), and in the valleys observed many warm springs which are said never to freeze in winter. I examined one, and found bubbles of gas rising to the surface.

We made an early start next morning, travelling E.N.E., and later in a more northerly direction. About noon, from a slight eminence, we could see a faint streak of blue over the trees; we travelled hard to reach it, and at sundown broke from the woods, shot down a steep bank, and stood on an immense snow-clad field of ice,—the mighty Yukon!

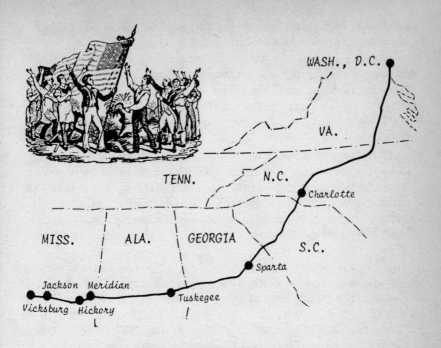

WASH., D.C.

VA.

TENN.

N.C.

Charlotte

MISS.   ALA.   GEORGIA

S.C.

Sparta

Jackson   Meridian

Tuskegee

Vicksburg   Hickory

THE MOST SENSATIONAL WALK
IN AMERICAN HISTORY

Two years after the Civil War, a Wisconsin man made the following bet with his buddies: "I bet I can walk the same route through the South General Sherman used, carry an unfurled Union flag at all times, live exclusively off Southern hospitality, and come to no harm." Here's how it turned out as described by Irwin Ross in THE OLD FARMER'S ALMANAC.

On a cold day in November, two and one-half years after the Confederacy had collapsed at Appomattox, four Yankee veterans sat arguing around the stove in the general store in Edgerton, Wisconsin. That argument led to a strange bet—and the most sensational walk any man ever took through American history.

In those bitter postwar days, the triumphant North was split. On one side were those who felt, like incumbent President Andrew Johnson, that all should be forgiven and forgotten. The other side, the haters, demanded vengeance through "get tough" policies, and threatened to impeach the President.

"We licked 'em, but has that changed 'em any?" argued the Edgerton storekeeper. "Traitors don't change."

"They're Americans, just like us," said Gil Bates, a former sergeant of the First Wisconsin Heavy Artillery. "I'll bet I could walk right through, say where Sherman marched to the sea, and nobody would touch me."

The others took him up on it, and the terms of the wager were these: Sergeant Gilbert H. Bates engages to walk from Vicksburg, Mississippi, to Washington, D.C., carrying the Union flag unfurled; to go unarmed and without bodyguard; to carry no money and accept none, but live off Southern hospitality, to start in January and finish, at the latest, by the following Fourth of July.

In the middle of January, 1868, the sergeant left on what his friends regarded as attempted suicide. Everybody knew that Johnny Reb had plenty of reason to hate the Yank. The South was devastated, parts of it close to famine.

For his friendly invasion of the South, Bates wore rough farmer's clothes. He was 30, square-shouldered, dark-haired, with deep-set blue-grey eyes and a natural courtesy of manner.

On the train for Vicksburg his seat-mate, a traveling salesman from Kentucky, inquired his business. Bates told him. He actually could give no clear idea of his purpose, which was nothing less than to prove the brotherhood of man, but his eyes shone with obvious honesty and faith.

At Vicksburg, the salesman insisted on putting the sergeant up at the Prentiss House. Being well known in the city, he did more. Bates had hardly washed up when the mayor and a committee of prominent citizens came calling.

Vicksburg took over Gil and his cause. The mayor gave him an official dinner. A group of young men had a velvet walking suit made to order for him—to his embarrassment. When he appeared on the streets he was cheered, his hand wrung.

To replace his tattered regimental flag, a delegation of ladies presented him with a fine new silk Star Spangled Banner they had sewed for him themselves. Tears came to his eyes as he accepted it. For the hands that had made it had only a short time before been sewing the Stars and Bars.

His departure for Jackson was a triumphal procession led by the mayor and councilmen on horseback. Next came a brass band, then Bates with his new flag, then people in carriages, then people on foot.

At the city limits he was cheered, his hand shaken, his back pounded. He waved his flag and started out, alone with the South now.

At three o'clock he reached the village of Bovina. The weather was raw and damp, with snow falling. The closed, dark houses looked hostile. The only person about was a stern, angry-seeming old gentleman who demanded to know, what he was up to, carrying the Union flag.

When Bates told him, the old gentleman took off his overcoat without a word, draped it over the sergeant's shoulders, stepped back, saluted, and marched off. Bates called after him. The old man wheeled, saluted again, turned a corner and disappeared.

At dark, Bates approached a ruined plantation house. Its owner came to the door and the sergeant found himself propelled inside, to tell his story over a brandy beside a roaring fire.

"You must stay the night," said Mr. Cordevent of Kidd's Plantation. "I apologize for the bareness of my hospitality. My broken windows and wrecked furniture are Northern improvements. No offense meant, suh. We'd have done the same to you if we'd had the chance."

Bates went on his way the next morning, warmed inside by Southern food and outside by a Southern overcoat. The snow had turned to cold rain. The roads were mud bogs and he took to the railroad tracks.

Some four miles from Smith Station, a train came to a stop beside him. The passengers swarmed out to shake his hand. They knew from Vicksburg the story of the crazy Yank with the Stars and Stripes.

Many offered money, which Bates refused. But as the train started, the conductor thrust some bills into his pocket, saying they were for postage stamps for letters back home—to tell the North that Southerners were "all-fired Americans."

At Edwards' Station, a cheering crowd welcomed him. In the midst of it, suddenly, Bates began to laugh. When he could stop, finally, he told how well-meaning friends in Wisconsin had warned him he would never come back alive, that the Southerners would cut out his heart and trample it on the flag. Men stamped and howled, and in laughter he set out again.

Jackson made Sergeant Bates the city's honored guest. He was warmly welcomed at the Capitol and forced to make a speech about his mission of American brotherhood. In an impromptu ceremony, he waved his flag from the balcony.

At a lonesome spot called Hickory, exhausted, rainsodden, Bates stopped for the night at the home of a Mr. Gray. His much-shaken hand, arm and shoulder were giving him pain, his feet were chafed, and the 12-pound flag needed drying out.

In the dead of night, he was awakened by the sound of many voices. He started up in alarm, and went to the window. In the light of torches, he made out about 50 men who shouted when they saw him. It sounded menacing—until he heard the gay music of "Arkansas Traveler" squealingly performed by a dozen fiddles.

He went out. The rain had stopped. He saw that the men had brought a keg of whiskey. "Some of us has come 40 miles to see you, Sarge," said one of them, handing him a tin cup full to the brim. "Here's to the flag." Bates sang and jigged with them until nearly daylight.

He took to the road again, feeling no weight at all in the flag he carried. At Meridian, he was paraded through the streets in an open carriage, his flag unfurled, while Southern belles waved their kerchiefs and blew kisses.

So it went on, this odyssey of a soldier passionately attached to his flag—as a symbol not of conquest but of peace.

At White Hall Plantation, while he was sleeping, the ladies decorated his banner with laurel wreaths. It was St. Valentine's day. On the road from Sparta he was ambushed—by a picnic party of children, school having been recessed to make him welcome. Farther on he was ambushed again, this time by 20 ladies who had been waiting for him, with a dinner all prepared.

Informed of a dying rebel captain who wanted to see him, Bates left his route for the first time. He left the road again when a woodchopper begged him to visit the grave of his brother, killed in the war. They prayed there together.

"Joyful multitudes everywhere hail his advance as though it were the advance of an Emperor," commented a *New York Times* editorial describing his progress. Gilbert Bates had proved that the Southern heart was sound; and the professional haters must certainly realize it by now.

In Charlotte, young James Orr came to him. "Sir, I was a soldier under Lee. Here is a flag of yours we took after hard fighting and many killed. You have recaptured it. Sergeant, without firing a shot—take it!"

In Tuskegee, he had a grand reception on the day after the House of Representatives voted to impeach the President. "Shook hands with every man in Columbia (South Carolina) today, I think, and with several of them more than once," he noted in his diary.

He found only one Southern newspaper hostile—*Pollard's Southern Opinion*, which called for the Carolinians "to meet you at the border, welcome your insolent approach, and seat you on some tall solitary chimney left by Sherman as a bleak monument of his vandal raid, and there let you wave your rag of oppression amid the hootings and curses of an insulted people."

At the border, 25 Confederate veterans awaited him—to escort him in honor into the state. On the same day, the United States Senate began sittings on the impeachment of the "appeasing" President.

Sergeant Bates arrived in Washington—and was met by the usual rain, crowds, cheers and a brass band—on April 14. A happy procession practically danced him to the Executive Mansion. President Johnson came on the front steps to greet him. Gilbert Bates' 1,400-mile mission was completed.

And the impeachment of President Johnson, when the votes were counted, failed, if by a narrow margin. But it never entered the mind of the man who quietly resumed his life in Wisconsin that it might have been his mission that saved the President. Nor is there any available proof that it did.

But the simple action of this plain man from the grass roots did prove that in spite of a bloody civil war, and its aftermath of grief, devastation and intrigues of politics, Americans were still all of one family.

EAST FROM CALIFORNIA BY RAIL

A train journey from San Francisco to Greeley, Colorado, just four years after the completion of the first transcontinental rail line, is among the many revealing commentaries on western America of a century ago to be found in the 1873 travel diary of a plucky English spinster named Isabella Lucy Bird. Returning alone from the Sandwich Islands to England, fortyish, indomitable Miss Bird decided to explore the scenic wonders of the Colorado Rockies, a feat which she accomplished largely on horseback and packing a pistol. Her rail trip, her many adventures on the raw frontier, and the unusual characters she encountered there were described in letters sent home to her sister Henrietta. First published in book form in 1879, with the title A LADY'S LIFE IN THE ROCKY MOUNTAINS, *these letters were often reprinted, most recently in 1960 by the University of Oklahoma Press. The following narrative depicting the pleasures and inconveniences of early rail travel is excerpted from the opening pages of the diary begun in early September of 1873.*

$\mathbb{I}$t is a weariness to go back, even in thought, to the clang of San Francisco, which I left in its cold morning fog early yesterday, driving to the Oakland ferry through streets with side-walks heaped with thousands of cantaloupe and water-melons, tomatoes, cucumbers, squashes, pears, grapes, peaches, apricots—all of startling size as compared with any I ever saw before. Other streets were piled with sacks of flour, left out all night, owing to the security from rain at this season. I pass hastily over the early part of the journey, the crossing the bay in a fog as chill as November, the number of "lunch baskets," which gave the car the look of conveying a great picnic party, the last view of the Pacific, on which I had looked for nearly a year, the fierce sunshine and brilliant sky inland, the look of long *rainlessness,* which one may not call drought, the valleys with sides crimson with the poison oak, the dusty vineyards, with great purple clusters thick among the leaves, and between the vines great dusty melons lying on the dusty earth. From off the boundless harvest fields the grain was carried in June, and it is now stacked in sacks along the track, awaiting freightage. California is a "land flowing with milk and honey." The barns are bursting with fullness. In the dusty orchards the apple and pear branches are supported, that they may not break down under the weight of fruit; melons, tomatoes, and squashes of gigantic size lie almost unheeded on the ground; fat cattle, gorged almost to repletion, shade themselves under the oaks; superb "red" horses shine, not with grooming, but with condition; and thriving farms everywhere show on what a solid basis the prosperity of the "Golden State" is founded. Very uninviting, however rich, was the blazing Sacramento Valley, and very repulsive the city of Sacramento, which, at a distance of 125 miles from the Pacific, has an elevation of only thirty feet. The mercury stood at 103° in the shade, and the fine white dust was stifling.

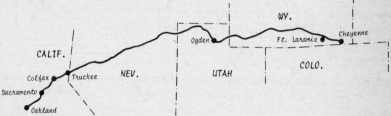

In the late afternoon we began the ascent of the Sierras, whose sawlike points had been in sight for many miles. The dusty fertility was all left behind, the country became rocky and gravelly, and deeply scored by streams bearing the muddy wash

111

of the mountain gold mines down to the muddier Sacramento. There were long broken ridges and deep ravines, the ridges becoming longer, the ravines deeper, the pines thicker and larger, as we ascended into a cool atmosphere of exquisite purity, and before six P.M. the last traces of cultivation and the last hardwood trees were left behind.

At Colfax, a station at a height of 2,400 feet, I got out and walked the length of the train. First came two great gaudy engines, the Grizzly Bear and the White Fox, with their respective tenders loaded with logs of wood, the engines with great, solitary, reflecting lamps in front above the cow guards, a quantity of polished brass-work, comfortable glass houses, and well-stuffed seats for the engine-drivers. The engines and tenders were succeeded by a baggage car, the latter loaded with bullion and valuable parcels, and in charge of two "express agents." Each of these cars is forty-five feet long. Then came two cars loaded with peaches and grapes; then two "silver palace" cars, each sixty feet long; then a smoking car, at that time occupied mainly by Chinamen; and then five ordinary passenger cars, with platforms like all the others, making altogether a train about 700 feet in length.

The light of the sinking sun from that time glorified the Sierras, and as the dew fell, aromatic odors made the still air sweet. On a single track, sometimes carried on a narrow ledge excavated from the mountain side by men lowered from the top in baskets, overhanging ravines from 2,000 to 3,000 feet deep, the monster train *snaked* its way upwards, stopping sometimes in front of a few frame houses, at others where nothing was to be seen but a log cabin with a few Chinamen hanging about it, but where trails on the sides of the ravines pointed to a gold country above and below. So sharp and frequent are the curves on some parts of the ascent, that on looking out of the window one could seldom see more than a part of the train at once. At Cape Horn, where the track curves round the ledge of a precipice 2,500 feet in depth, it is correct to be frightened, and a fashion of holding the breath and shutting the eyes prevails, but my fears were reserved for the crossing of a trestle bridge over a very deep chasm, which is itself approached by a sharp curve. This bridge appeared to be overlapped by the cars so as to produce the effect of looking down directly into a wild gulch, with a torrent raging along it at an immense depth below.

Shivering in the keen, frosty air near the summit pass of the Sierras, we entered the "snow-sheds," wooden galleries, which for about fifty miles shut out all the splendid views of the region, as given in dioramas, not even allowing a glimpse of "the Gem of the Sierras," the lovely Donner Lake. One of these sheds is twenty-seven miles long. In a few hours the mercury had fallen from 103°to:19°, and we had ascended 6,987 feet in 105 miles! After passing through the sheds, we had several grand views of a pine forest on fire before reaching Truckee at 11 P.M. having traveled 258 miles.

At Truckee Miss Bird rented a hotel room, next morning located a livery stable, then spent two days exploring the surrounding country on horseback, solo and wearing a unique riding habit that included ankle-length bloomers. After a frightening confrontation with a bear, and other adventures, she changed trains and continued to Cheyenne, Wyoming, her last stop before entering Colorado, where much of her story is laid.

Precisely at 11 P.M. the huge Pacific train, with its heavy bell tolling, thundered up to the door of the Truckee House, and on presenting my ticket at the double door of a "Silver Palace" car, the slippered steward, whispering low, conducted me to my berth—a luxurious bed three and a half feet wide, with a hair mattress on springs, fine linen sheets and costly California blankets. The twenty-four inmates of the car were all invisible, asleep behind rich curtains. It was a true Temple of Morpheus. Profound sleep was the object to which everything was dedicated. Four silver lamps hanging from the roof, and burning low, gave a dreamy light. On each side of the center passage, rich rep curtains, green and crimson, striped with gold, hung from silver bars running near the roof, and trailed on the soft Axminster carpet. The temperature was carefully kept at 70°. It was 29° outside. Silence and freedom from jolting were secured by double doors and windows, comely and ingenious arrangements of springs and cushions, and a speed limited to eighteen miles an hour.

As I lay down, the gallop under the dark pines, the frosty moon, the forest fires, the flaring lights and roaring din of

113

Truckee faded as dreams fade, and eight hours later a pure, pink dawn divulged a level blasted region, with grey sage brush growing out of a soil encrusted with alkali, and bounded on either side of low glaring ridges. All through that day we traveled under a cloudless sky over solitary glaring plains, and stopped twice at solitary, glaring frame houses, where coarse, greasy meals, infested by lazy flies, were provided at a dollar per head. By evening we were running across the continent on a bee line, and I sat for an hour on the rear platform of the rear car to enjoy the wonderful beauty of the sunset and the atmosphere. Far as one could see in the crystalline air there was nothing but desert. The jagged Humboldt ranges flaming in the sunset, with snow in their clefts, though forty-five miles off, looked within an easy canter. The bright metal track, purpling like all else in the cool distance, was all that linked one with Eastern or Western civilization.

The next morning, when the steward unceremoniously turned us out of our berths soon after sunrise, we were running down upon the Great Salt Lake, bounded by the white Wahsatch ranges. Along its shores, by means of irrigation, Mormon industry has compelled the ground to yield fine crops of hay and barley; and we passed several cabins, from which, even at that early hour, Mormons, each with two or three wives, were going forth to their day's work . . . . At the Mormon town of Ogden we changed cars, and again traversed dusty plains, white and glaring, varied by muddy streams and rough, arid valleys, now and then narrowing into canyons. By common consent the windows were kept closed to exclude the fine white alkaline dust, which is very irritating to the nostrils. The journey became more and more wearisome as we ascended rapidly over immense plains and wastes of gravel destitute of mountain boundaries, and with only here and there a "know" or "butte" to break the monotony. The wheel-marks of the trail to Utah often ran parallel with the track, and bones of oxen were bleaching in the sun, the remains of those "whose carcasses fell in the wilderness" on the long and drouthy journey. The daybreak of to-day (Sunday) found us shivering at Fort Laramie, a frontier post dismally situated at a height of 7,000 feet. Another 1,000 feet over gravelly levels brought us to Sherman, the highest level reached by this railroad. From this point eastward the streams fall into the Atlantic. The ascent of these apparently level plateaus is called "crossing the Rocky Mountains," but I have seen nothing of the range, except two peaks like teeth lying low on the distant horizon. It became mercilessly cold; some people thought it snowed, but I only saw rolling billows of fog. Lads passed through the cars the whole morning, selling newspapers, novels, cacti, lollypops, pop corn, pea nuts, and ivory ornaments, so that, having lost all reckoning of the days, I never knew that it was Sunday till the cars pulled up at the door of the hotel in this detestable place (Cheyenne).

Miss Bird found Cheyenne of 1873 a raw, rough place, made safe only by an alert Vigilance Committee. From her hotel window she witnessed the busy come-and-go of a typical frontier outpost.

Below the hotel window freight cars are being perpetually shunted, but beyond the railroad tracks are nothing but the brown plains, with their lonely sights—now a solitary horseman at a traveling amble, then a party of Indians in paint and feathers, but civilized up to the point of carrying firearms, mounted on sorry ponies, the bundled-up squaws riding astride on the baggage ponies, then a drove of ridgy-spined, long-horned cattle, which have been several months eating their way from Texas, with their escort of four or five much-spurred horsemen, in peaked hats, blue-hooded coats, and high boots, heavily armed with revolvers and repeating rifles, and riding small wiry horses. A solitary wagon, with a white tilt, drawn by eight oxen, is probably bearing an emigrant and his fortunes to Colorado.

Afoot and light-hearted I take to the open road,
Healthy, free, the world before me,
The long brown path before me leading wherever I choose.

Henceforth I ask not good-fortune, I myself am good-fortune,
Henceforth I whimper no more, postpone no more,
    need nothing,
Done with indoor complaints, libraries, querulous criticisms,
Strong and content I travel the open road.

—From "Song of the Open Road," by Walt Whitman

104 POUNDS OF GOLD

*A young Texas cowman and his heavily-loaded money belt
negotiate 130 miles of outlaw-infested country in this tale related to
J. Frank Dobie by W. B. Slaughter and retold by Dobie in his book*
THE MUSTANGS.

Many years ago a little old cowman named W. B.
Slaughter who had once owned great herds but who, then broke,
was coming to the end of his life in San Antonio, told me this
story.

"Early in 1873, before grass had started, my brother J. B.
Slaughter and I came down from north Texas to Mason County
and contracted for 1500 head of big steers at $16 around, spring
delivery. I was twenty-three years old and had already bossed
two herds up the trail to Kansas. My brother was just nineteen.
From the day we signed the contract, cattle prices began going
up. By the date agreed on for delivery, the middle of April, those
steers were worth ten dollars a head more than the contract
price. When we got to Mason with our outfit to receive the steers
and start up the trail, we found a downhearted, sullen set of
cowmen. If they could break the contract, they would make
$15,000, and they were the kind of men to break a contract if they
could.

" 'Have you got the cash?' they asked.

"We showed them a letter of credit from a Dallas bank for
$50,000. They laughed at it. That was not money. There was a
little private bank in the town of Mason. We took the letter of
credit there. It didn't have more than a thousand dollars in the
vault. The banker couldn't help us. The stage for San Antonio
had just driven into town. I took it. We had three or four days left
to produce the cash.

"Colonel Breckenridge was the main banker in San Antonio.

116

He told me what kind of money belt to buy. Then he helped me pack $25,000 in ten- and twenty-dollar gold pieces into it. When the gold was all packed away, the belt weighed 104 pounds. I weighed around 135. I went to a second-hand store and bought the sorriest-looking hat and the most run-down pair of boots in stock. I went to one of the horse pens and picked out a pony that to some people would look disgraceful. He was a dunnish roan, tough and wiry. I paid $15 for him. I saddled him with an old hull that cost $5.

"Towards sundown I set out. The rough Llano River country across Mason County was at that time the hide-out place for as hard a set of outlaws as Texas ever had. There were so many of them and they were so bold that two years later the rangers rounded up every human male of that section into a stockade and cut the sheep out from the goats, just as you would cut cattle. The good men had nothing to fear and were glad to be rid of the others. On the straightest possible road, it is about 115 miles from San Antonio to Mason. My route was across the open range west of the stage road. It must have covered over 130 miles. If I met any stranger I was to pass as a green youth from Gonzales looking for a job with a trail herd. My purpose was not to meet anybody, especially men on the watch—for I was expected with the cash.

"By daylight I had covered something less than half the distance. I stopped close to water and staked my horse in a little opening enclosed by brush. Then I crawled into the brush and slept. Of course I had a sixshooter. At dark I saddled up and rode on north. About every two hours I'd unsaddle and let my horse graze. He wallowed once or twice. Lots of the time he traveled in a lope. By sunup I was getting close to Mason. Instead of riding straight into town, I circled it and came in from the north. I learned later that the stage from San Antonio had been carefully looked over by some strange men several miles down the road.

"Well, when we planked down the gold, those ranchers had to take it. The Mason banker didn't want it, and I guess the ranchers got it to San Antonio all right. Nobody in that country wanted any money about his premises. I threw that little yellow-roan pony in with our remuda and just north of Red River we sold him and the other cow horses along with the steers at $28 around."

JOHN MUIR WALKS
AMONG THE SEQUOIA

We who enjoy the benefits of our national conservation program owe much to John Muir, the Scotch-American explorer, naturalist and writer who spent many years campaigning for forest conservation. He was instrumental in the passage of the Yosemite National Park Bill in 1890, establishing both Yosemite and Sequoia national parks.

From his youth in Wisconsin Muir was a great walker and lover of nature. He kept notebooks during his travels and published several books, including THE STORY OF MY BOYHOOD AND YOUTH, A THOUSAND-MILE WALK TO THE GULF *and* OUR NATIONAL PARKS. *An excerpt from the latter is included here, in which Muir describes with sincere reverence his first intensive study of the sequoia belt of the Sierra Nevada of California in 1875.*

One of my own best excursions among the Sequoias was made in the autumn of 1875, when I explored the then unknown or little known Sequoia region south of the Mariposa Grove for comprehensive views of the belt, and to learn what I could of the peculiar distribution of the species and its history in general. In particular I was anxious to try to find out whether it had ever been more widely distributed since the glacial period; what conditions favorable or otherwise were affecting it; what were its relations to climate, topography, soil, and the other trees growing with it, etc.; and whether, as was generally supposed, the species was nearing extinction. I was already acquainted in a general way with the northern groves, but excepting some passing glimpses gained on excursions into the High Sierra about the head-waters of King's and Kern Rivers I had seen nothing of the south end of the belt.

Nearly all my mountaineering has been done on foot, carrying as little as possible, depending on camp-fires for warmth, that so I might be light and free to go wherever my studies might lead. On this Sequoia trip, which promised to be long, I was persuaded to take a small wild mule with me to carry provisions and a pair of blankets. The friendly owner of the animal, having noticed that I sometimes looked tired when I came down from the peaks to replenish my bread-sack, assured me that his "little Brownie mule" was just what I wanted, tough as a knot, perfectly untirable, low and narrow, just right for squeezing through brush, able to climb like a chipmunk, jump from boulder to boulder like a wild sheep, and go anywhere a man could go. But tough as he was and accomplished as a climber, many a time in the course of our journey when he was jaded and hungry, wedged fast in rocks or struggling in chaparral like a fly in a spiderweb, his troubles were sad to see, and I wished he would leave me and find his way home alone.

We set out from Yosemite about the end of August and our first camp was made in the well-known Mariposa Grove. Here and in the adjacent Pine woods I spent nearly a week, carefully examining the boundaries of the grove for traces of its greater extension without finding any. Then I struck out into the majestic trackless forest to the southeastward, hoping to find new groves or traces of old ones in the dense Silver Fir and Pine woods about the head of Big Creek, where soil and climate seemed most favorable to their growth, but not a single tree or old monument of any sort came to light until I climbed the high rock called Wamellow by the Indians. Here I obtained telling views of the fertile forest-filled basin of the upper Fresno. Innumerable spires of the noble Yellow Pine were displayed rising above one another on the braided slopes, and yet nobler Sugar Pines with superb arms outstretched in the rich autumn light, while away toward the southwest, on the verge of the glowing horizon, I discovered the majestic dome-like crowns of Big Trees towering high over all, singly and in close grove congregations.

Day after day, from grove to grove, cañon to cañon, I made a long, wavering way, terribly rough in some places for Brownie, but cheery for me, for Big Trees were seldom out of sight. We crossed the rugged, picturesque basins of Redwood Creek, the North Fork of the Kaweah, and Marble Fork gloriously forested, and full of beautiful cascades and falls, sheer and slanting, infinitely varied with broad curly foam fleeces and strips of embroidery in which the sunbeams revel. Thence we climbed into the noble forest on the Marble and Middle Fork Divide. After a general exploration of the Kaweah basin, this part of the Sequoia belt seemed to me the finest, and I then named it "the Giant Forest." It extends, a magnificent growth of giants grouped in pure temple groves, ranged in colonnades along the sides of meadows, or scattered among the other trees, from the granite headlands overlooking the hot foot-hills and plains of the San Joaquin back to within a few miles of the old glacier-fountains at an elevation of 5000 to 8400 feet above the sea.

Resting awhile on one of the most beautiful of [the meadows] when the sun was high, it seemed impossible that any other forest picture in the world could rival it. There lay the grassy, flowery lawn, three fourths of a mile long, smoothly outspread, basking in mellow autumn light, colored brown and yellow and purple, streaked with lines of green along the streams, and ruffled here and there with patches of ledum and scarlet vaccinium. Around the margin there is first a fringe of azalea and willow bushes, colored orange-yellow, enlivened with vivid dashes of red cornel, as if painted. Then up spring the mighty walls of verdure three hundred feet high, the brown fluted pillars so thick and tall and strong they seem fit to uphold the sky; the dense foliage, swelling forward in rounded bosses on the upper half, variously shaded and tinted, that of the young trees dark green, of the old yellowish. An aged lightning-smitten patriarch standing a little forward beyond the general line with knotty arms outspread was covered with gray and yellow lichens and surrounded by a group of saplings whose slender spires seemed to lack not a single leaf or spray in their wondrous perfection. Such was the Kaweah meadow picture that golden afternoon, and as I gazed every color seemed to deepen and glow as if the progress of the fresh sun-work were visible from hour to hour, while every tree seemed religious and conscious of the presence of God. . . .

MOVING DAY FOR THE SECOND

*Traveling some 350 miles through an Indian-infested wilderness
was all in the day's work for the dependents of both officers and
enlisted men of the Second United States Cavalry a century ago. In
the late summer of 1877 word had gone out that the regiment, most
of its units scattered at various Wyoming posts, was to rendezvous
at Medicine Bow, about 100 miles northwest of Cheyenne. Troopers,
the regimental band, baggage wagons, and camp followers were to
gather there and proceed to two new forts being built in Montana.*

*The following account of the Second's adventure-filled journey,
which began on September 2 at Medicine Bow, was written by D. J.
O'Malley, at the time a ten-year-old boy whose stepfather, Charles
White, recently had enlisted in Troop E. After a boyhood spent
around cavalry mounts, O'Malley worked as a Montana cowboy for
nineteen years, spent much of his later life at Eau Claire, Wisconsin, working in a factory turning out rubber tires for the machine
that made the horse virtually a collector's item. He wrote many
historical articles and poems on cowboy life for Montana newspapers. "Moving Day for the Second" appeared in the* ROCKY MOUNTAIN
HUSBANDMAN, *Great Falls, on July 2, 1936.*

Immediately after breakfast Sept. 2 a trumpeter sounded the call to break camp, and everyone sprang into action. Tents began to fall and were rolled and tied; camp property was put into shape and loaded [into wagons that would also carry the soldiers' families].

About 9 o'clock the trumpet sounded assembly and the different troops fell into position. Then came the call "Mount," and they were in the saddle and the march started.

I cannot recall the different places at which we camped, but the first sign of habitation was Fort Fetterman on the Platte river. This fort was situated on a high hill close to the river and commanded a view of the surrounding country. Here the command met its first trouble. The Platte is a treacherous stream full of quicksand and holes. We were nearly all day fording it.

Two teams were drowned, as was one of the soldiers who became entangled in the chains and harness of the drowning mules.

We stayed in camp all the next day and the drowned soldier was buried at the fort. The two wagons were recovered from the river and put in shape again. After leaving Fetterman, orders were issued that only one move a day would be made and camp was usually made around 2 P. M.

As soon as a place was found suitable for a camp the picket guard was placed, two or three soldiers in a place, on the highest ground within a mile of the camp. I remember one afternoon about four days out from Fetterman, all stock had been brought in, cavalry horses were tied to their temporary picket line, mules were tied at their wagons. Numerous children were playing in front of the tents when all of a sudden they heard the trumpeter at the guard tent sound that significant call, "Boots and Saddles." Instantly the camp was a scene of excitement. The soldiers sprang from their tents to their horses. The women and children were hurried to the center of the camp where the heavy wagons were always parked in a hollow square for their protection. Then assembly sounded; a troop surrounded the square where the women and children were and the rest formed in line and advanced toward where the picket had reported a body of horsemen. We could see the troop halt and then two troops advanced in a skirmish line.

The skirmish line had gotten about 600 yards in advance of the main body of troops when up on a little ridge where the picket had been stationed who gave the alarms, rode a bunch of 25 horsemen. One of our guard said, loud enough so some of heard him, "There they come all right," and then added quickly, "Say, they've got a guidon. It's soldiers," and it was. It was a detachment of mounted infantry from Fetterman who had been sent after us with some orders for the colonel of our command.

Before the command reached Wind river, signs of Indians were noticed and skirmish lines were thrown out twice but no live Indians put in their appearance. Once three dead bodies were found on scaffolds built in the branches of cottonwoods. On investigation it was found they were Sioux and had not been dead long. Double pickets were put out and double guards placed at night.

About eight miles from Wind river we crossed a fresh trail which evidently had been made by a large band of Indians, who appeared to be traveling in the same direction we were. The command was ordered into camp as soon as we reached water and a troop was sent to follow the trail and report any sign of Indians. They followed the trail for 10 miles when it swung to the northwest. They found no Indians except a dead one in a tree. The scout with the troop said he thought the trail was at least three days old. We found out after we reached Fort Keogh that a bunch of about 400 Sioux had made that trail and had been engaged by troops from Fort Ellis and captured.

The next camp of any note that I remember was at old Fort Phil Kearny on the Piney. This fort had been harassed by Red Cloud and his fighting Sioux about 1867 until it was abandoned by the government and the troops were barely out of sight of the fort when the Indians had every building burning. It was at or near Kearny that Colonel Fetterman and his command were killed by the Sioux in 1867.

We camped just below the old fort. The charred remnants of a good many of the old buildings could be plainly seen. The fort was built of logs, and much of the old charred logs were used by our command for their kitchen fires. We stayed in the camp two days as there was plenty of wood and water and grass for the stock. The afternoon of the first day, one of the soldiers of C troop who was on herd guard, came near causing mutiny in the regiment and also among the teamsters. While the horses were on water he got off his horse to get himself a drink and noticed in a gravel riffle quite a quantity of what he thought was gold dust. He managed to secure about a teaspoonfull of it which he put in a tin tobacco box, and when he got to camp he showed it to some of the troops and told them the creek was full of it. The news soon spread over the camp and it was with difficulty the soldiers were restrained from going in a body to get the gold. It took a show of arms to hold them and several of the soldiers who had had experience in placer mining, convinced the gold-eager men that the stuff was mica, or as it was commonly called, "Fool's Gold," and was not worth a dollar a ton.

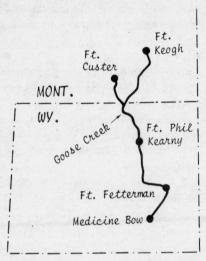

The second fatality of the trip occured when camped at Goose creek.

It was found that there was plenty of fish in Goose creek and permission was given the troops to catch some. One party of soldiers made a makeshift seine out of gunny sacks and was meeting with fair success. While they were dragging the seine in a bend of the creek where the water was deep, one of the soldiers stepped into a deep hole and went out of sight. He failed to come to the surface and the others attempted to find him. He was found in 10 minutes, about 25 feet below where he had disappeared and was caught in the roots of some old drift logs beneath the surface.

From Goose creek we moved to Prairie Dog creek and went into camp for a couple of days and we could see that some new arrangements were being made and it was found that the command would move in two parts when we left. Part of the troops and transportation were to go to Fort Custer [on the Big Horn just north of the Custer Battlefield, and part to Fort Keogh near the present site of Miles City]. A, B, E, and I troops were the ones to be stationed at Fort Keogh. The balance of the regiment with the band, went to Fort Custer, which was to be the headquarters of the Second cavalry, Fort Keogh being the headquarters of the 5th Infantry.

The troops for Custer began their journey the third morning after we had pitched camp on Prairie Dog and the Keogh contingent were to leave the following morning. That night it was found that the wife of trumpeter Clancy of troop E was about to give birth to a baby and could not possibly be moved for about a week. A new problem faced our commanding officer. It was decided to leave our doctor and a detachment of soldiers at that camp while the command went to Keogh from where an ambulance and other transportation were to be sent back for them. The commanding officer called for a volunteer from among the women to stay with the sick woman and though there were about 25 married women in our camp, my mother was the only one who volunteered to stay. A detachment of 25 men under command of my step-father, Charles White, was left to guard camp. [There were six children—four Clancys, my sister, and myself.] It was with misgivings that the little group watched the rest leave. We were alone in a wild country overrun with hostile Indians and no one knew when a war party would show up. Mrs. Clancy's baby was born that night. White divided his small command into two guards. One guarded camp during the day and one at night. It seemed to me as though he (White) was on guard all the time. He seemed to be up at all times of the day and night.

The evening of the sixth day after the troops had left us, we heard the sound of a military trumpet from down the creek sound "Halt." White, who was at the tents, ordered Clancy to sound "Advance," and the entire camp was alive. In a minute or so, from across the creek came a body of horsemen followed by a Red Cross ambulance and two four mule jerk-line teams. It was a detachment of soldiers from Keogh who had come for us. One of the fort doctors, R. G. Redd, was with them, and they had medicine for the sick. Camp was lively that evening. We children had a fine time with the new soldiers who were from the Fifth infantry. They were mounted on captured Indian horses. Two of them were of our own troops who had been sent with them as guides. Dr. Redd found that Mrs. Clancy was in condition to be moved and the next day we started for Fort Keogh. Mother went in the ambulance with Mrs. Clancy, while we children were placed in the wagons carrying camp equipment. We moved a lot faster now than we did with the main command. After we struck Tongue river the country was smoother and the cavalry and all the wagons that had preceeded us were kept on a trot whenever practical.

About 2 o'clock p.m. Oct. 5, 1877, we came in sight of Fort Keogh, our future home. We surely were an excited band of boys and girls. We made all sorts of conjectures as to where we were going to live and what we were going to do, and could hardly wait for the mules (who now seemed to us to be creeping along) to get us to the fort. We went directly to the new fort which was not yet entirely built, and the tents for the two laundresses of troop E, my mother and Mrs. Clancy, were pitched about 200 yards east of the troop quarters. We stayed in tents all winter as no quarters had been built for the enlisted men's wives as yet. But all the fine double frame buildings for the officers and their families were about completed. Each married soldier had two 10 x 14 wall tents to live in. These were pitched, one directly in front of the other and both topped by a large government tarpaulin. They proved to be comfortable and we lived in ours until the following spring, when log houses were put up for the laundresses.

UP THE TRAIL IN '79

Many a Texan first viewed the Great Plains of the Far West from the hurricane deck of a Texas cowpony while driving a herd of Long-horn beeves overland from the Lone Star State to markets further north. One such who committed his unusual experience to writing was 19-year-old Baylis John Fletcher, member of a crew of eight cowboys and a cook under trail boss George Arnett who left Victoria, Texas, on April 11, 1879, with about 2,000 cattle, bound for Cheyenne, Wyoming, more than a thousand miles away. They reached their destination on August 15.

The story of Fletcher's four months in the saddle, written by him in 1912, long after the events chronicled, is among the best of the eye-witness accounts of trail drives. First published, serially, in 1966, by the monthly magazine THE CATTLEMAN, *it was issued in book form by the University of Oklahoma Press in 1968. The following excerpt from* UP THE TRAIL IN '79, *with its surprise ending, is a graphic picture of rapidly changing conditions on the prairies of western Kansas a century ago.*

We crossed the Cimarron again right at the line of Kansas. We were informed that this was the last water we should find until we reached the Arkansas at Dodge City, more than a hundred miles away. The waters of the Cimarron were good at this point, and we watered our herd freely before starting the long drive. We filled our water barrel to the brim, but we started out for a hundred miles without stock water. We had not been averaging more than twelve miles a day, but now we must exceed that rate or our animals would die of thirst before we could reach the Arkansas. [The figure of 100 miles appears to be an error. It probably should be about 60, as the statement "four days later" in the next paragraph indicates.]

Four days later, on the glorious Fourth of July, we came in sight of the Arkansas River. We had lost no cattle, but they were staggering along in a line for at least five miles up and down the trail. The stronger had outtraveled the weaker, and the herd was pulled in two, forming two distinct droves. Fortunately, there had been showers in the Arkansas Valley south of Dodge City, forming small ponds that enabled the cattle gradually to slake their thirst before they reached the river. Otherwise, we might have lost some cattle from overdrinking.

We now got into trouble through ignorance of Kansas customs. We had never traveled in a country with herd laws. Not dreaming that any man would try to grow a crop of grain without fencing his land, we let our whole herd of 1,700 cattle invade the wheat field of a homesteader. He drove us out with dogs and lurid oaths, but when he was informed of our ignorance, he laughed and said he would excuse us this time but that we must not repeat the experiment.

We bought a fresh supply of provisions at Dodge City, including a keg of pickles. During the entire trip we had tasted no vegetables other than beans or "prairie strawberries" as some called them, and when the pickles were opened, the men would eat nothing else until they were all devoured.

Dodge was said to be the wickedest town in the West at that time, but we saw little of its wickedness. Our stay in town was limited to a few hours each, and that during the day. No cowpuncher was permitted to stay in town at night. Among the curiosities I saw at the station were great piles of buffalo bones awaiting shipment. They were enormous, with the skulls of many of the big bulls still decorated with the short, thick horns peculiar to the buffalo.

After our shopping was done, we forded the Arkansas River and kept well to the north through western Kansas. The plains were high now, and all watercourses flowed through deep canyons. There were scattered settlements made by homesteaders. The settlers lived chiefly in dugouts, excavations in the sides of canyons, with roofs thatched with grass and then covered with turf. Sometimes we saw houses built of prairie sod as it was turned by the plow and cut in sections like building stones. We were told that in these semi-arid regions sod houses lasted for years.

On one occasion, as we were guiding our weary herd along the trail, the big steers that always led the herd saw a heap of earth and ran bellowing to it. They began to paw it with their forefeet and to toss the turf with their horns. We were unaware that they were destroying a human habitation until a woman came running out from an opening in the ground and fighting the steers frantically with her sunbonnet. When she called on us to drive the cattle away, we hastened to the rescue, but it was too late. The roof of the dugout was caved in and the frontier home ruined. Again we pleaded ignorance, but with no more success than at Dodge City. The woman was greatly exasperated by the partial destruction of her dugout. We offered our services to help rebuild it, but she disdainfully declined them, declaring that persons who were so ignorant as to allow their cattle to destroy the dugout could do little toward repairing it. We were extremely sorry, but we could not gain her forgiveness.

Passing on, we were met by a band of homesteaders mounted on mules and brood mares, all bareback and some barefoot. They approached us in a body and informed us that we must turn to the west, as they had settled on the trail directly north from us and would not allow any Texas cattle to be driven through their settlement. Texas fever, they declared, scattered Texas-fever germs, and the fever would kill their domestic cattle. There was no alternative but to yield to their wishes. We were not prepared to make a forcible invasion of Kansas but must do as directed. So, turning out of our trail, we made a detour of about fifteen miles to go around this settlement.

Not far from this place we found a lone herder running a trail hospital. From several herds, crippled and disabled cattle had been cut out into a hospital bunch and left with this young man to be cared for until they should be able to travel.

We now crossed the Kansas Pacific Railroad at Buffalo Parks station, noted as the place where two bandits of the famous Big Springs train robbery had been killed less than two years earlier.

On the afternoon of the first day after leaving Buffalo Parks station, we met a man riding across the plain, stopping at intervals to survey the horizon with a field glass. His movements excited our curiosity, and when he came up to us and asked whether we had seen any Indians, we became deeply interested. He said it was rumored that the Cheyennes had left their reservation at Fort Supply in the Indian Territory and had gone on the warpath. It was said that they were following the cow trail to their hunting grounds in Dakota. The rumor further credited them with having killed and scalped a number of settlers in western Kansas. We knew that during the summer of 1878, just one year before, the Cheyennes had made a raid through Kansas and Nebraska, massacring many homesteaders. Later in the afternoon we met several more scouts who told the same story as the lone horseman.

Just before sunset we entered a deep canyon through which flowed a small stream which we were told was a tributary of the Republican River. While we were selecting a camping spot for the night, another scout arrived, claiming to have recent news. He said that the Cheyennes in a large body had crossed the railroad just west of Buffalo Parks on the preceding night and that they were headed north. They must be hiding in some of the deep canyons in our immediate vicinity. He cautioned us to look out for a raid that night. We found some dry driftwood along the creek, and for the first time in many weeks we built a big wood fire by which to eat our evening meal. The cattle had been bedded down about a quarter of a mile farther up the canyon, and three men were guarding them.

As we were quietly eating our supper, these three cowboys dashed up to our camp and said that a large body of horsemen, presumably Indians, were crossing the canyon just above our camp. George Arnett sprang to his feet and called for three volunteers to go with him to reconnoiter. Poinsett Barton, Dick Russell, and I joined him. Arming ourselves, we rode quietly by the dim starlight to the sleeping cattle, then beyond them to the west for half a mile, but we saw no man. We rode up the steep canyon walls to the level plain and halted while Mr. Arnett, who was an old Indian fighter, dismounted and put his ear to the ground. He heard the distant tramping of a large body of horses. We all dismounted then and scanned the horizon of the level plain.

Silhouetted against the northern sky, we saw what appeared to be a large body of horses, or horsemen, rapidly receding in the distant gloom. They might be renegade savages, but if so they had passed us and it would be madness to pursue them. So we followed the rim of the canyon until we were opposite our campfire. Just as we turned to descend, we heard the sound of horses' hoofs and we saw the dim outline of a man on horseback chasing our saddle horses. "Don't shoot!" shouted Mr. Arnett as one of our number brought his carbine to bear on the rider. "I think it's Al Cochran driving the horses." On returning to camp, we found that he was right. The boy had driven the horses up to the wagon.

After reporting the result of our reconnaissance, Mr. Arnett said, "Now, boys, I don't think there is a particle of danger tonight, for the strangers, whoever they are, have crossed the creek and are rapidly leaving us. They will not return. But if any of you are uneasy, we can safely leave the herd and the wagon and go up the canyon a mile or so and remain concealed for the night. The cattle will not run off, and there are no range cattle to mix with them. If no Indians come, the cattle and horses will be safe. If they do come in such force as reported, we shall be powerless to resist them. I do not believe all these Indian tales, but I leave it to you as to what we shall do tonight."

After some discussion, during which I could not help recalling some of Aunt Ellen's stories of Indian massacres, we took a vote and, by an overwhelming majority, decided to leave camp for the night. So we replenished the campfire and filed quietly away on our night horses up the canyon of the creek. Finding a secluded spot hedged in by wild currant bushes, we dismounted and placed a sentinel on guard at the top of the canyon's side. We staked our horses with their saddles on. At regular intervals during the night the sentinel was relieved of his picket duty. Nothing disturbed the silence on the plain during the night except the occasional howl of a coyote.

On the following morning we returned to camp, where we found nothing molested. The cattle had scattered a little, but soon we had them rounded up and ready for the trail. There was no trace of savages. After breakfast we resumed our march up the trail. We soon came to a trail leading to the garrison at Oberlin. It was lined with homesteaders and their families, all in a state of panic from the Indian tales. Some of the women and girls were weeping and some were laughing, but all were flying for their lives to get within the shelter of the soldiers' guns at Oberlin. Scouts were riding over the plains with field glasses, trying in vain to locate the Indians. For several days the panic continued. As we approached the dugouts of the homesteaders, we found them deserted. We no longer had any trouble from settlers who might try to turn us away from our course. No one molested us. In fact, the people seemed glad for our presence. But where were the bloodthirsty Cheyennes?

At last we came to the south prong of Sappa River. There, grazing in the valley, was a herd of about eight hundred horses and a full outfit of cowboys herding them. The outfit was from Texas, and the horses were being trailed to Ogallala, Nebraska, to supply the demand for cow ponies on the big ranches. The boss of the horse herd approached us with a bland smile. After exchanging greetings, he asked, "Seen any Indians?"

"No," we replied, "but we have heard of them every day. What does all this mean?"

"Well," said the horse driver, "we were so harassed by the settlers driving us from place to place that we had to resort to some expedient to make us welcome intruders. They would not let us pass through their settlements and would not let us rest to graze our horses, so we had to do something. We began making night drives and putting out Indian reports. The raid of last year was fresh in memory, and all we had to do to depopulate the plains was to start Indian tales. In our night drives during the dark of the moon, we were mistaken for a strong band of Cheyennes. We are the only Indians in western Kansas, but please keep mum. If they get onto our joke, they will come back and hang us every one. We passed your herd one night on the north prong of the Solomon River. Did you take us for Indians, too?"

It was all plain to us now. We were innocent of the trickery, but we had shared in the benefits of the panic. The unscrupulous old frontiersman who bossed the horse herd knew the source of that hospitality characteristic of border inhabitants when there is danger of savage foes. He had succeeded in making himself welcome by exciting the gravest fears among people unused to the dangers of frontier life. They were all settlers from the East and were easily thrown into a panic by a suggestion of Indians. He had resorted to a heroic treatment for selfishness and had worked a marvelous cure. But, as he said, the secret must be kept until he was at a safe distance from the victims of this faked scare.

THEODORE ROOSEVELT IN COWBOY LAND

Theodore Roosevelt was a member of the New York State Assembly in 1883 when he bought an interest in North Dakota cattle ranches. He wrote in his autobiography, "I do not believe there ever was any life more attractive to a vigorous young fellow than life on a cattle ranch in those days." After the Presidential campaign of 1884, Roosevelt saw no immediate opportunity for usefulness in politics, and he again journeyed to the Elkhorn Ranch near Medora, where he spent most of the next two years sharing in all the work and living "the strenuous life" of a ranchman and cowboy. These passages from his autobiography describe incidents in his involvement in the wilderness of the West.

Though I had previously made a trip into the then Territory of Dakota, beyond the Red River, it was not until 1883 that I went to the Little Missouri, and there took hold of two cattle ranches, the Chimney Butte and the Elkhorn.

It was still the Wild West in those days, the Far West, the West of Owen Wister's stories and Frederic Remington's drawings, the West of the Indian and the buffalo-hunter, the soldier and the cow-puncher. That land of the West has gone now, "gone, gone with lost Atlantis," gone to the isle of ghosts and of strange dead memories. It was a land of vast silent spaces, of lonely rivers, and of plains where the wild game stared at the passing horseman. It was a land of scattered ranches, of herds of long-horned cattle, and of reckless riders who unmoved looked in the eyes of life or of death. In that land we led a free and hardy life, with horse and with rifle. We worked under the scorching midsummer sun, when the wide plains shimmered and wavered in the heat; and we knew the freezing misery of riding night guard round the cattle in the late fall round-up.

Night guards for the cattle herd were assigned by the captain of the wagon, or perhaps by the round-up foreman, according to the needs of the case, the guards standing for two hours at a time from eight in the evening till four in the morning. The first and last watches were preferable, because sleep was not broken as in both of the other two. If things went well, the cattle would soon bed down and nothing further would occur until morning, when there was a repetition of the work, the wagon moving each day eight or ten miles to some appointed camping-place.

Each man would picket his night horse near the wagon, usually choosing the quietest animal in his string for that purpose, because to saddle and mount a "mean" horse at night is not pleasant. When utterly tired, it was hard to have to get up for one's trick at night herd. Nevertheless, on ordinary nights the two hours round the cattle in the still darkness were pleasant. The loneliness, under the vast empty sky, and the silence, in which the breathing of the cattle sounded loud, and the alert readiness to meet any emergency which might suddenly arise out of the formless night, all combined to give one a sense of subdued interest. Then, one soon got to know the cattle of marked individuality, the ones that led the others into mischief; and one also grew to recognize the traits they all possessed in common, and the impulses which, for instance, made a whole herd get up towards midnight, each beast turning round and then lying down again. But by the end of the watch each rider had studied the cattle until it grew monotonous, and heartily welcomed his relief guard.

One night there was a heavy storm, and all of us who were at the wagons were obliged to turn out hastily to help the night herders. After a while there was a terrific peal of thunder, the lightning struck right by the herd, and away all the beasts went, heads and horns and tails in the air. For a minute or two I could make out nothing except the dark forms of the beasts running on every side of me, and I should have been very sorry if my horse had stumbled, for those behind would have trodden me down. Then the herd split, part going to one side, while the other part seemingly kept straight ahead, and I galloped as hard as ever beside them. I was trying to reach the point—the leading animals—in order to turn them, when suddenly there was a tremendous splashing in front. I could dimly make out that the cattle immediately ahead and to one side of me were disappearing, and the next moment the horse and I went off a cut bank into the Little Missouri. I bent away back in the saddle, and though the horse almost went down he just recovered himself, and, plunging and struggling through water and quicksand, we made the other side. Here I discovered that there was another cowboy with the same part of the herd that I was with; but almost immediately we separated. I galloped hard through a bottom covered with big cottonwood trees, and stopped the part of the herd that I was with, but very soon they broke on me again, and repeated this twice. Finally toward morning the few I had left came to a halt.

It had been raining hard for some time. I got off my horse and leaned against a tree, but before long the infernal cattle started on again, and I had to ride after them. Dawn came soon after this, and I was able to make out where I was and head the cattle back, collecting other little bunches as I went. After a while I came on a cowboy on foot carrying his saddle on his head. He was my companion of the previous night. His horse had gone full speed into a tree and killed itself, the man, however, not being hurt. I could not help him, as I had all I could do to handle the cattle. When I got them to the wagon, most of the other men had already come in and the riders were just starting on the long circle. One of the men changed my horse for me while I ate a hasty breakfast, and then we were off for the day's work.

As only about half of the night herd had been brought back, the circle riding was particularly heavy, and it was ten hours before we were back at the wagon. We then changed horses again and worked the whole herd until after sunset, finishing just as it grew too dark to do anything more. By this time I had been nearly forty hours in the saddle, changing horses five times, and my clothes had thoroughly dried on me, and I fell asleep as soon as I touched the bedding. Fortunately some men who had gotten in late in the morning had had their sleep during the daytime, so that the rest of us escaped night guard and were not called until four next morning. Nobody ever gets enough sleep on a round-up.

Of course amusing incidents occurred now and then. Usually these took place when I was hunting lost horses, for in hunting lost horses I was ordinarily alone, and occasionally had to travel a hundred or a hundred and fifty miles away from my own country. On one such occasion I reached a little cow town long after dark, stabled my horse in an empty outbuilding, and when I reached the hotel was informed in response to my request for a bed that I could have the last one left, as there was only one other man in it. The room to which I was shown contained two double beds; one contained two men fast asleep, and the other only one man, also asleep. This man proved to be a friend, one of the Bill Joneses whom I have previously mentioned. I undressed according to the fashion of the day and place, that is, I put my trousers, boots, shaps, and gun down beside the bed, and turned in. A couple of hours later I was awakened by the door being thrown open and a lantern flashed in my face, the light gleaming on the muzzle of a cocked .45. Another man said to the lantern-bearer, "It ain't him"; the next moment my bedfellow was covered with two guns, and addressed, "Now, Bill, don't make a fuss, but come along quiet." "I'm not thinking of making a fuss," said Bill. "That's right," was the answer; "we're your friends; we don't want to hurt you; we just want you to come along, you know why." And Bill pulled on his trousers and boots and walked out with them. Up to this time there had not been a sound from the other bed. Now a match was scratched, a candle lit, and one of the men in the other bed looked round the room. At this point I committed the breach of etiquette of asking questions. "I wonder why they took Bill," I said. There was no answer, and I repeated, "I wonder why they took Bill." "Well," said the man with the candle, dryly, "I reckon they wanted him," and with that he blew out the candle and conversation ceased. Later I discovered that Bill in a fit of playfulness had held up the Northern Pacific train at a near-by station by shooting at the feet of the conductor to make him dance. This was purely a joke on Bill's part, but the Northern Pacific people possessed a less robust sense of humor, and on their complaint the United States Marshal was sent after Bill, on the ground that by delaying the train he had interfered with the mails.

The only time I ever had serious trouble was at an even more primitive little hotel than the one in question. It was also on an occasion when I was out after lost horses. Below the hotel had merely a bar-room, a dining-room, and a lean-to kitchen; above was a loft with fifteen or twenty beds in it. It was late in the evening when I reached the place. I heard one or two shots in the bar-room as I came up, and I disliked going in. But there was nowhere else to go, and it was a cold night. Inside the room were several men, who, including the bartender, were wearing the kind of smile worn by men who are making believe to like what they don't like. A shabby individual in a broad hat with a cocked gun in each hand was walking up and down the floor talking with strident profanity. He had evidently been shooting at the clock, which had two or three holes in its face.

He was not a "bad man" of the really dangerous type, the true man-killer type, but he was an objectionable creature, a would-be bad man, a bully who for the moment was having things all his own way. As soon as he saw me he hailed me as "Four eyes," in reference to my spectacles, and said, "Four eyes is going to treat." I joined in the laugh and got behind the stove and sat down, thinking to escape notice. He followed me, however, and though I tried to pass it off as a jest this merely made him more offensive, and he stood leaning over me, a gun in each hand, using very foul language. He was foolish to stand so near, and, moreover, his heels were close together, so that his position was unstable. Accordingly, in response to his reiterated command that I should set up the drinks, I said, "Well, if I've got to, I've got to," and rose, looking past him.

As I rose, I struck quick and hard with my right just to one side of the point of his jaw, hitting with my left as I straightened out, and then again with my right. He fired the guns, but I do not know whether this was merely a convulsive action of his hands or whether he was trying to shoot at me. When he went down he struck the corner of the bar with his head. It was not a case in which one could afford to take chances, and if he had moved I was about to drop on his ribs with my knees; but he was senseless. I took away his guns, and the other people in the room, who were now loud in their denunciation of him, hustled him out and put him in a shed. I got dinner as soon as possible, sitting in a corner of the dining-room away from the windows, and then went upstairs to bed where it was dark so that there would be no chance of any one shooting at me from the outside. However, nothing happened. When my assailant came to, he went down to the station and left on a freight.

LAST DAY WITH THE DOGIES

The final day of a trail drive is depicted in these verses by Western poet-historian Joseph Mills Hanson, a native of Yankton, South Dakota. A saddle-weary crew has been on the go for weeks, perhaps even for months, pushing a herd of Longhorns north from Texas to a railroad shipping point in Kansas or Nebraska. This day starts like any other, but in the late afternoon, as a ramshackle little railroad town and its sprawling wooden cattle pens show up on the horizon, there is a feeling of exhilaration. The cantankerous dogies will soon be someone else's responsibility and the cowpunchers will be free to celebrate for a night or two before starting for the home ranch.

Written to fit the tune of the old Scottish air "Bonnie Dundee," the Hanson poem was first printed in LESLIE'S MAGAZINE *for October 1904 with the title "Cowboy Song." Since then it has appeared in dozens of song books, virtually always without credit to the author, under the title "The Railroad Corral."*

We are up in the morning ere dawning of day
And the grub wagon's busy and flap-jacks in play;
While the herd is astir over hillside and swale
With the night-riders rounding them into the trail.

Come, take up your cinches
And shake up your reins;
Come, wake up your broncho
And break for the plains;
Come, roust those red steers from the long chaparral,
For the outfit is off for the railroad corral!

The sun circles upward, the steers as they plod
Are pounding to powder the hot prairie sod
And, it seems, as the dust turns you dizzy and sick
That you'll never reach noon and the cool, shady creek.

But tie up your kerchief
And ply up your nag;
Come, dry up your grumbles
And try not to lag;
Come, larrup those steers from the long chaparral,
For we're far on the way to the railroad corral!

The afternoon shadows are starting to lean
When the grub wagon sticks in a marshy ravine
And the herd scatters further than vision can look
For you bet all true punchers will help out the cook!

So shake out your rawhide
And snake it up fair;
Come, break your old broncho
To taking his share!
Come, now for the steers in the long chaparral,
For it's all in the drive to the railroad corral!

But the longest of days must reach evening at last,
When the hills are all climbed and the creeks are all passed
And the tired herd droops in the yellowing light;
Let them loaf if they will, for the railroad's in sight!

So flap up your holster
And snap up your belt;
Come, strap up the saddle
Whose lap you have felt;
Good-by to the steers and the long chaparral!
There's a town that's a trump by the railroad corral!

THE "FAREWELL TRIP"

One day in 1935, Ernie Pyle gave up his comfortable desk job as managing editor of the Washington Daily News to take off on a nearly non-stop journey of five years that would carry him back and forth and up and down the country and into every state at least three times, writing a daily newspaper article. The following report about a famous railroad trip that ended in disaster is from a chapter in HOME COUNTRY, *a sampling of his best writings during those years.*

Ernie Pyle left his "home country" during World War II to report, in his unpretentious, personal style, from the fighting fronts in Europe and the Pacific. He was shot and killed in April 1945.

I suppose the most famous railroad engineer who ever pulled a throttle was John Luther Jones, better known as "Casey." Nearly everybody in America has sung that song—how Casey "mounted to his cabin with his orders in his hand, and took his farewell trip to that promised land." But did you know that Casey Jones was a real person, who was actually killed in a railroad wreck? I had a long talk in Memphis with Casey's fireman, who went through the wreck with him. He was a colored man named Sim Webb. He was sixty-two, tall and slender, and his skin was light brown. His kinky hair was grayish, but his face was thin and young-looking.

The wreck happened at Vaughan Station, in Mississippi, just before daylight on the morning of May 1, 1900. Sim Webb could tell you the exact minute of nearly every mile of that last wild ride of Casey's. He had told it so many times that he reeled off stations and minutes and speeds with the sureness of a mental calculator.

Sim Webb was twenty-six at the time, and Casey Jones was thirty-two. Sim had been firing for Casey only four months. They were pulling a fast passenger train, on a run from Memphis to Canton, Mississippi. They were due out of Memphis at 11:30 P.M., but on the fatal night the connecting train was delayed and they were an hour and a half late getting out. But "Mr. Casey" was in high spirits, so Sim poured on the coal and Casey bent the throttle back and they boiled south through the night, making up time. They went so fast that when they hit the freight, with just twelve miles to go, they were running only two minutes behind time.

Somewhere around a quarter to four, with the cab a bedlam of noise and rushing air, and the miles clicking off every fifty seconds or so, Casey looked at his watch, and stood up and yelled across the boilertop to Sim: "Sim, the old girl's got her high-heeled slippers on tonight." Those were his last words.

The wreck wasn't Casey's fault; it was the fault of a freight train that had taken the siding, leaving several cars sticking out onto the main line.

"We were going around a double-S curve," Sim Webb said. "We had taken the curve on Mr. Casey's side, and then we swung around so the curve was on my side. All of a sudden I saw the caboose ahead of us. Mr. Casey couldn't see it from his side. I jumped up and yelled, 'Look out, we're gonna hit something.' I never heard him say anything. I just know he stood up, and I heard him kick the seat out from under him. I grabbed the handrail and swung myself down and out of the cab. I held to the rail till I was almost down to the ground, and then let go. Just missed a cattle gate by that far. I hit the ground at seventy-five miles an hour. When I woke up I was in a hospital. The engine went clear through the caboose, through a car of corn, through a car of hay, and stopped in a car of lumber, but it stayed on the track. It was stripped clean—cab and everything stripped off. They found Mr. Casey's body in the clear, lying on the ground by the back trucks. Every bone was broken. Mr. Casey was a fine man."

As soon as he was out of the hospital, Sim went back to firing on the same run. He went through another bad wreck during the flood time in 1918. A trestle gave way and the locomotive toppled off and fell on its side into the river. The engineer was thrown clear, but Sim went under with the engine. Somehow he managed to fish his way out of the cab and get to the top. He had a cigar stub in his mouth when they left the tracks, and it was still in his mouth when he came up. His family kept at him to quit the railroad, so in 1919 he gave in and became a bricklayer. In his new, safe trade a wall caved in on him, covered him with six feet of rock, broke his leg, and put him in the hospital for two months.

RAILROAD WRECKS IN AMERICAN BALLADS

Railroad wrecks are soon forgotten unless some balladeer perpetuates the story in song. If Casey Jones is number 1 on the list of ballads about train wrecks, then "The Wreck of the Old 97" is probably the second-best known.

On September 27, 1903, Number 97, a fast mail of the Southern Railway, was an hour behind schedule when a fresh engineer, Joseph A. Broady, took over the throttle at Monroe, Virginia. Engineer Broady accepted the challenge to make up the time and sent Old 97 hurtling down a hill toward Stillhouse Trestle, a lofty, spidery structure crossing a creek near Danville. The roadbed curved sharply just before the trestle, and Old 97 couldn't hang onto the rails as it sped around the bend. Over she went — locomotive and five cars — plunging into the stream bank and carrying some ten railroad employees and postal clerks to their deaths.

And the brave engineer, Joseph Broady? Well, he was found dead in the wreck, but, in the best tradition of railroading, "with his hand on the throttle."

A resident of the area arrived at the scene while the wreck was still smoldering. Impressed with the drama, he composed a poem, set it to the tune of a favorite melody, and thus immortalized "The Wreck of the Old 97."

RIDING TO TOWN

Ohio-born Paul Laurence Dunbar was the first black American to express in distinguished poetry the feelings of his people. "Riding to Town" is from his book LYRICS OF LOWLY LIFE *issued in 1896.*

When labor is light and the morning is fair,
I find it a pleasure beyond all compare
To hitch up my nag and go hurrying down
And take Katie May for a ride into town;
   For bumpety-bump goes the wagon,
     But tra-la-la-la our lay.
There's joy in a song as we rattle along
   In the light of the glorious day.

A coach would be fine, but a spring wagon's good;
My jeans are a match for Kate's gingham and hood;
The hills take us up and the vales take us down,
But what matters that? we are riding to town,
   And bumpety-bump goes the wagon,
     But tra-la-la-la sing we.
There's never a care may live in the air
   That is filled with the breath of our glee.

And after we've started, there's naught can repress
The thrill of our hearts in their wild happiness;
The heavens may smile or the heavens may frown,
And it's all one to us when we're riding to town.
   For bumpety-bump goes the wagon,
     But tra-la-la-la we shout,
For our hearts they are clear and there's nothing to fear,
   And we've never a pain nor a doubt.

The wagon is weak and the roadway is rough,
And tho' it is long it is not long enough,
For mid all my ecstasies this is the crown
To sit beside Katie and ride into town,
   When bumpety-bump goes the wagon,
     But tra-la-la-la our song;
And if I had my way, I'd be willing to pay
   If the road could be made twice as long.

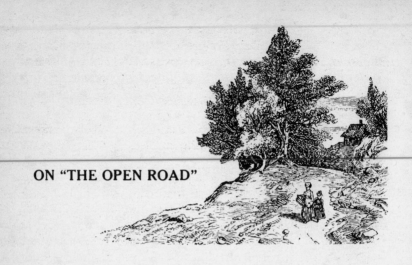

ON "THE OPEN ROAD"

In an autobiography entitled MIDSTREAM, *Helen Keller relates her experiences on "The Open Road" during lecture tours which took her all over America. Miss Keller's accounts of these journeys are most remarkable because she never saw nor heard anything which she describes with such sensitivity and accuracy.*

At the age of 18 months Helen Keller was stricken with an illness which left her permanently deaf and blind. As a result of her deafness, she also became dumb. For five years she was confined by these handicaps. Then, in 1887, Anne Sullivan, a graduate of the Perkins Institution for the Blind at Boston, was engaged to bring the world to little Miss Keller. The amazing progress these two people made together is one of the great stories of human achievement. Miss Keller gradually learned a manual alphabet, lip reading by touch, reading braille, writing and speaking. She graduated, cum laude, from Radcliffe College.

During the autumn of 1913 we were for the first time constantly on the road. It was pleasant to find myself generally known, and people glad to come to hear me, but it was hard to accustom myself to the strangeness of public life. At home I had always been where I could breathe the woodland air. My life had been as it were "between the budding and the falling leaf," and I had felt along my veins the thrill of vine and blossom. Winter and spring had brought me wind-blown messages across marsh, brook, and stonewalled field. I had felt

> God's great freedom all around,
> And free life's song the only sound.

All such peaceful, expansive sensations cannot be enjoyed in the throbbing whirl of a train, the rattle of lurching taxis, or the confinement of hotels and lecture halls.

But after a while I learned to enjoy the rhythmic vibration of the train as it sped over long distances. In the swift, steady motion my body found rest, and my mind kept pace with the stretch of the horizon and the ever shifting clouds. I could not tell which interested me most, the excitement of departure from a city, or the rush over great plains and undulating country, or the arrival at the next lecture with hope of accomplishment in my heart.

Our travels were a queer jumble of dull and exciting days.

I recall an amusing ride we had in the state of Washington on a sort of interurban car, which we called the "Galloping Goose" on account of its peculiar motion. It resembled a goose in other ways, too. It stopped when there was no reason for stopping; but we did not mind, as it was a lovely day in spring, and we got out and picked flowers by the side of the track.

Another time, when we were criss-crossing northern New York, it was necessary for us, in order to fill our engagement, to take an early morning train that collected milk. It was a pleasant experience. We literally stopped at every barn on the way. The milk was always waiting for us in tall, bright cans, and cheerful young farmers called out greetings to the trainmen. The morning was beautiful. It was a joy to have the country described to me. The spring foliage was exquisite, and I could picture the cows standing knee-deep in the luscious young grass which I could smell. They said the apple trees in bloom were a vision of loveliness.

Once we happened to be on the last train going through the flooded districts of Texas and Louisiana. I could feel the water beating against the coaches, and every now and then there was a jolt when we hit a floating log or a dead cow or horse. We caught an uprooted tree on the iron nose of our locomotive and carried it for quite a distance, which reminded me of the lines in "Macbeth":

> Macbeth shall never vanquish'd be, until
> Great Birnam wood to high Dunsinane hill
> Shall come against him.

and I wondered if it was a good or a bad omen. It must have been a good one; for we arrived at our destination many hours late, but safe and very thankful.

The first tour was typical of all our subsequent ones. In the years that followed we journeyed up and down the immensity of America from the storms of the Atlantic to the calms of the Pacific, from the Pine State to the Gulf States, along the banks of muddy creeks or following the Mississippi until it seemed to me as if we were tearing our way through life just like that tameless river.

Those tours are a symbol to me of the ceaseless travelling of my soul through the uplands of thought. My body is tethered, it is true, as I follow the dark trail from city to city and climate to climate; but the very act of going satisfies me with the feeling that my mind and body go together. It is a never-ending wonder for me how my days lead to

> . . . the start of superior journeys,
> To see nothing anywhere but what you may reach it
>   and pass it,
> To conceive no time however distant, but what you may reach
>   it and pass it,
> To look up and down no road but it stretches
> And waits for you, however long but it stretches and waits
>   for you, . .
> To gather the minds of men out of their brains as
>   you encounter them, to gather the love out of their hearts,

and

> to know the world itself as a road, as many roads to hope, as
>   roads for travelling souls.

That is why Walt Whitman's "The Open Road" is one of my favourite long poems, it holds up to me so faithfully a mirror of my own inner experience.

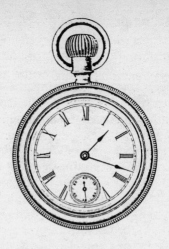

STANDARD TIME, AN AMERICAN INVENTION

Prior to 1883, long-distance train travel was complicated by the lack of any systematic way of reckoning time. Cities and towns used local sun time. Each railroad chose the time that suited it best, and its conductors and stationmasters set their watches and clocks accordingly. A New York Central R.R. clock in Buffalo, for example, would show New York City time, about twenty minutes *ahead* of local sun time. A Michigan Southern R.R. clock in Buffalo would show the time at Columbus, Ohio, some fifteen minutes *behind* local time. A similar time puzzle faced the traveler in any other city served by more than one railroad. Making connections was often an adventure.

Much of the credit for getting something done about such chaos goes to a minister, Charles F. Dowd, head of a ladies' seminary at Saratoga Springs, New York. In 1869, concurrently with the completion of the first transcontinental railway, orderly-minded Rev. Dowd began a one-man crusade for a logical time system. He envisioned a world theoretically divided into twenty-four time zones, each including fifteen degrees of longitude, the distance the sun appears to travel from east to west in one hour. In any given zone, all the clocks would show the same time.

So convincing were the Rev. Dowd's arguments and writings that leading scientific societies also began applying pressure for time reform. Eventually the railroads of the United States and Canada capitulated and adopted Standard Time as we know it today. The herculean task of adjusting the schedules of more than fifty different railway systems to the new method of time-keeping fell to the publisher of *The Official Railway Guide*, William F. Allen, whose work is commemorated by a large bronze plaque on an inside wall of Washington's Union Station.

The change-over took place, amid great excitement, on Sunday, November 18, 1883. As telegraphers in New York, on a signal from the Naval Observatory at Washington, flashed noon to other cities across the continent, the hands of all the clocks in Buffalo and elsewhere throughout the Eastern Time Zone were moved to 12 o'clock. In the Central Zone the official time became 11 o'clock, in the Mountain Zone 10 o'clock, in the Pacific Zone 9 o'clock. Timepieces everywhere chimed together on the hour for the first time in history.

Other nations quickly realized the advantages of Standard Time. In 1884 delegates from twenty-six countries met in Washington to discuss it and Standard Time was soon extended virtually to the rest of the globe.

Neither the railroads nor a supposedly grateful public ever got around to erecting a monument to the Rev. Charles F. Dowd. Ironically, he was killed by a train at Saratoga Springs in 1904 at the age of seventy-nine.

—John I. White

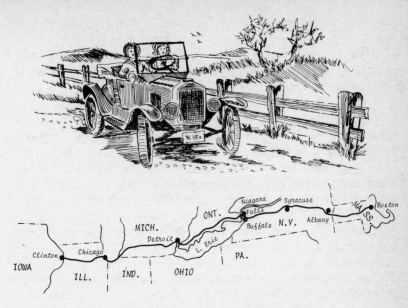

A LONG WAY FROM BOSTON

If any one automobile ushered in the age of family motoring, it was Henry Ford's Model T. Most people didn't venture too far, but Beth O'Shea and Kit Crandall drove all the way across the continent to California and a good part of the way back in Henrietta, their Model T, in the early 1920's. Henrietta finally expired in New Orleans, and the two adventurers finished their return to Boston on a coastwise steamer.

Many years later, Beth O'Shea wrote a charming story about their experiences, and in the following selections we learn much about the joys and sorrows of automobile travel a half century ago.

Stanley Bishop, my boss at Stafford's Store, was full of little maxims.

"All you dip up is a bucketful," he used to quote. "The larger the bucket the more you get out of the well."

He meant, of course, that one should increase one's capacity for enjoyment. One should take courses—learn to appreciate good literature, good art and good music. Kit and I were never the ones for courses, but during our first spring in Boston, something happened which enlarged our buckets considerably.

Kit had gone home to spend her Easter vacation in Vermont, and the afternoon she got back she called me at the store.

"I'll meet you when you're through work," she said, "I've got a surprise."

When I got out at six I had my first look at Henrietta, as we coyly christened her. She was a 1918 Model-T Ford roadster, painted black. As she sat high at the curb, with her stubby hood, her short wheel base and her rakish top, she looked like what those early cars really were—a carriage that had mislaid its horse. The engine was chugging contentedly, causing the little automobile to tremble like a bowl of aspic.

"I drove it down myself," Kit said proudly. "Passed the driver's test and got the license without any trouble at all."

I climbed in and we drove down Tremont Street and out Boylston while she explained how she had fallen heir to such a prize. Her mother, the only woman driver in town, had used it for four years to get to committee meetings and sewing circles. Then Mary and Mal Prescott, on their first visit from California since their marriage, had bought Mrs. Crandall a shiny new Cadillac, and Kit had inherited Henrietta. It was certainly a stroke of luck, for a car of one's own was an unheard-of luxury for girls of our age in those days.

Coming back along the Charles River, Kit stopped at the foot of our steep little street.

"I guess I'd better not try to drive up it," she decided. "The engine might stall."

We laughed about that later when we were negotiating the switch-back grades through the Rockies, but at the time, I was quick to urge her not to attempt anything so hazardous as Beacon Hill. I remembered too well those Sunday trips through the White Mountains in an old Jackson, when everybody would hold his breath hoping it would make a big hill in low gear. If it didn't, the car started slipping backward, giving us the sickening sense of being out of control entirely and headed for the ditch. The driver would pull up the emergency brake with a mighty heave, and then everybody else would pile out and put rocks behind the wheels to hold it until it could be started again.

Henrietta, as we were to learn, seldom slipped backward on

hills. She was very light and she had a good deal of power for her size. But on that first day we didn't know her very well and hadn't the slightest notion of what went on beneath her hood. We parked her in a Charles Street garage and walked up to our rooming house, full of plans about the rides we'd take on the spring Sundays to come.

A car certainly did open up the world. We saw the battlefields of Lexington and Concord. We drove over to the Charlestown slums to look at Bunker Hill and down to Plymouth to view the famous Rock. We even ventured as far as Provincetown on the tip end of Cape Cod.

I can't remember at just what point we began talking about driving across the continent. I'm sure the idea was mine originally, for I was always reading Walt Whitman, Bliss Carmen, Vachel Lindsay and all that company of vagabonds who sang nostalgically of the open road and far horizons. It was Kit, on the other hand, who got the maps and did the figuring on backs of envelopes about the number of miles per gallon. It was she who said, "Let's do it. Let's start May 31." That date coincided with the close of her school year.

I'm afraid I hedged a little when I saw my dream being abruptly translated into terms of action. Perhaps we should think about it a while longer—save some more money....

"If you want to do a thing," Kit said flatly, "the only way is to do it. If you wait, you'll never go."

We expected opposition and nobody can say we didn't get it. In the first place, it wasn't done. Maybe a couple of fellows could do it as a stunt, but not two girls alone. There was the danger— the kind of people we'd be meeting, the unsettled condition of the country after the war, the "Red Menace," the lack of suitable accommodations, the bad roads....

"The bears?" Kit suggested flippantly.

"And the Indians?" I put in.

They said it wasn't any joke. There would very likely be bears and Indians, and maybe wolves. We thought so, too, but we weren't going to worry about them until they were actually breathing down our necks.

What did worry us was the question of money. Although we had been brought up in the thrifty tradition of putting by a little each week, we had less than a hundred dollars apiece in our savings accounts.

"Vachel Lindsay," I pointed out, "started out on the road without a penny. He used to stop at houses and sell his rhymes for bread."

Kit didn't think that sounded very practical and anyhow, what would we use for rhymes? Eventually, we decided upon aprons—frilly affairs made of cretonne. They were called bungalow aprons and housewives were supposed to like to put them on in the afternoon. For eighteen dollars and sixty-five cents, we bought three dozen from a wholesaler who had come to the store, and planned to sell them at a profit to farm women who couldn't get to town to buy their own. That, we thought optimistically, would take care of our food and keep gas and oil in Henrietta.

Next, we consulted the American Automobile Association about routes, and they recommended the Lincoln Highway. The Santa Fe Trail, they said, would be full of snow so early in the spring, but the Lincoln should be in pretty good shape they thought. Of course there would be plenty of bad spots on either, for the big road-building project was only just getting under way throughout the West, and they warned that, in some states gas stations were seventy-five miles apart and there were practically no hotels.

Well—we couldn't afford hotels anyway, except once in a while when we'd sold a lot of aprons. Mostly we would camp out—"spread our blankets under the stars" as I said dreamily. Our camping experience so far had been confined to toasting hot dogs with the Girl Scouts, but that didn't deter us. We could learn, couldn't we?

Accordingly, we began to assemble our wardrobes and equipment. Those were the days before slacks, so we bought khaki riding breeches, leather coats and sweaters. Although my fellow workers at the store made no secret of their disapproval of the trip, they surprised us by coming through with a half-dozen shirts—flannel and pongee—a basket of fruit and, to express the proper note of pessimism, a well-stocked first-aid kit. We considered taking a tent and rejected that because there would be no place to stow it, but we got a rubber tarpaulin and some army blankets. As for the collapsible water buckets, shovels, tow ropes, axes and pulleys they said we would need, we scorned them all on the theory that we'd cope with trouble as we came to it, and never look more than a car-length ahead.

When all was ready, Kit stepped on the starter and the engine burst into an immediate roar, as it always did when there was a good mechanic standing by. The garage door was rolled open and we were off, trundling out into Charles Street and setting the course south by west.

The little streets were shining in the sun, there was a morning mist on the river, and the grass up in Louisburg Square was growing green. Boston looked very quiet and tranquil and safe all at once, and we didn't know when we would be seeing it again.

The gift shops all the way from Boston to California used to display among the sentimental framed verses a little gem called "Out Where the West Begins." According to the poet, you knew you had reached the West when you began to notice that the sun was shining more strongly and that hearts were beating with a correspondingly greater warmth.

Kit and I never were sure just where the West began for us, but there was no question that, during the first week of the trip, we carried Boston right along with us. The Lincoln Highway, a smooth black ribbon winding over hill and dale, rolled gently through the Berkshires, and Henrietta gave no trouble at all. Hour after hour she kept to her top speed which was forty miles with a good tailwind. The towns slid by, with their elm-shaded lawns and pleasant houses—just like the New England towns and houses we had known all our lives. Albany, Syracuse, Buffalo. We gave them our polite but unenthusiastic interest and dug down into the common travel fund to pay for nights in their clean hotels. Evenings we went sedately to the movies and saw Charlie Chaplin, Douglas Fairbanks, Gloria Swanson or Clara Bow. Sometimes we saw Tom Mix or Bill Hart and wondered if the cowboys, when we came to them, would actually wear those enormous hats and high-heeled boots.

"When we get out West," we kept saying, "we'll really rough it." When the West began, we would start camping, we would stop at farmhouses and sell aprons, we would have adventures. In the meantime we were not pioneers following in the wake of the prairie wagons. We were just two ladies from Boston out for a ride. We were self-conscious about stopping even to ask directions, we were uncomfortable in our unfamiliar clothes and, though we wouldn't admit it, we sometimes had a bleak suspicion that everyone else had been right and that the expedition was a silly idea. It had been exciting bucking the opposition and asserting our right to freedom, but the expected thrilled reaction at being actually on our way didn't come at first. Instead there was a definite let-down.

We were getting on each other's nerves, too, and that was distressing for, in the whole six months we had lived together in Boston, we never had had a quarrel. Kit annoyed me because she was always figuring mileage.

"Two hundred miles a day," she would say. "At this rate we could make the Coast in two weeks."

"Who wants to make the Coast in two weeks?" I would ask crossly.

"I do—if I have to do all the driving."

My driving had become a sore subject to both of us, for the first day's lesson had proved that I was never going to be a good natural driver as Kit was. Although it is generally agreed that the Model-T was the simplest mechanism ever devised by an automobile manufacturer, it never was simple to me. My feet were always getting mixed up among the three pedals and my finger, hooked around the hand throttle on the steering wheel, failed to function at the proper time so that we would go into reverse at odd moments or leap forward into a ditch with a mighty lunge.

It was my fault, too, that we got lost so frequently. I had refused flatly to take along one of those motor bibles called Blue Books, remembering them too well from the autombile trips of my childhood. "Turn left at the covered bridge," they used to say, "go on two miles to the four forks and bear right by the red barn." Whoever had the seat of honor beside the driver got the Blue-Book job and spent the day with his nose glued to the fine-typed pages and read aloud each direction, but never quite in time to prevent the wrong turn. Without a Blue Book we not only took the wrong turns; we frequently kept on wrong roads for miles before we discovered our mistake. That always made Kit furious. How were we going to make Utica that night if we had to spend time doubling back on the trail?

"And why do we have to make Utica tonight?" I would ask.

"After all we've got all summer."

Our first experience with bad roads came on the fifth day out when we made our ill-advised detour through Ontario. At Niagara, after we had put on slickers and gone behind the Falls with the honeymooners and other tourists, we learned that there were two ways to get to Detroit. One was the Lincoln Highway that we had been following all along; the other, which nobody ever used they said, was on the Canadian side with dirt roads all the way.

All afternoon we followed a road that ran parallel to Lake Erie but never quite reached it. The dust billowed around us in dense clouds, a burning wind blew constantly across the fields, and the maple trees withered in the heat.

Soon Henrietta's tires began to pop like firecrackers, and we learned the art of changing them by the process of trial and error. Theoretically, we understood the way it was done, but always at home there had been a garage handy when an occasional blow-out came, so we never had had actual practice.

First came the jack which refused to take a firm grip on the axle and slipped off every time the car seemed to be rising satisfactorily into the air. Then we had to pry loose the rusted clincher shoe. After that we were ready for that false friend, the Benedict Arnold of early motorists, the "Jiffy Repair Kit."

"You fix the patch," Kit directed, "while I get the tube ready."

That meant that she smoothed the wound with a nutmeg grater, while I smeared on the cement and when she gave the signal, pressed home the patch.

"That's that," I sighed with satisfaction, but of course it wasn't. We still had to wait by the roadside for twenty minutes while it "set" and after that came the back-breaking job with the tire pump.

It took at least forty minutes to change a tire, and we changed five that afternoon. Something went wrong with the starter, too, so each time we started, we had to crank.

That night, as we limped aboard the ferry which would take us back to the States and civilization, a boy on the boat pointed to the rear left tire. "It's flat," he said, and it was so pleasant to be spoken to again that it sounded almost like good news. We drove into Detroit on the rim and stopped at the first restaurant we came to. Fortified with large American steaks, we felt better able to tackle another patching job, but we didn't have to. When we got back to Henrietta we found an interested group gathered around her.

"Ain't you girls scared to come so far west?" one man asked.

Presently we found ourselves sitting on the curb telling them all about the trip while they fixed the tire. Canada hadn't been much fun, but judging from the way they laughed, it seemed to make a good story afterward.

You'll be all right on the Lincoln as far as Chicago, but after that . . ." This announcement was invariably followed by an expressive shrugging of shoulders, and we gathered that we would then take off into uncharted wilderness. To our surprise, however, the road continued wide and well kept up to the Iowa state line and beyond.

The first day out of Chicago was bright and windy. The buffalo peas were blooming in pink and purple masses, and the meadow larks were singing straight at the sun. Hatless and sunburned, and feeling recklessly gay and relaxed, we skimmed along in our well-behaved Henrietta . . . .

We made our first camp near Clinton on a bank of the Mississippi. It was twilight when we came to the big river, and men in shantyboats were net fishing in the brown water tinged with the pink of sunset.

As we drove along the river road, the fireflies were beginning to twinkle in the gathering dusk, and over on the sandbar some boys were swimming, their voices floated across to us. After a while we came to a large field where an old flivver touring car was parked in a grove of cottonwoods, and a man and a woman were sitting in camp chairs before a fire.

"Suppose they'd mind if we camped here too?" Kit wondered.

"Is this a tourist camp?" I asked, looking around with interest. We had heard about them, but had expected something more elaborate.

"Sure, it's a tourist camp," he told us. "Anythin's a tourist camp what has water and no no-trespass signs. All the towns has got 'em now. They figure they give you a place where you can pitch your tent and you'll buy food and stuff at their stores. You gals want I should give you a hand with your tent?"

They were both surprised when they learned we hadn't one. They'd run into a lot of boys traveling light like that, they said, but we were the first girls. "But you'll make out all right," Maw assured us. "They say it's real comfortable sleepin' on the ground once you git the trick of it. Me, I like a cot myself, but I'm not so young as I used to be."

Often in camps we'd run into the same people over and over again, and they grew to seem like old friends. They would worry if we didn't show up at the place they thought we should make by evening, and sometimes they'd even wait at some particularly bad stretch of road to make sure we got through all right.

In the evenings, around the fires, we would exchange information about routes, prices of food and gas, and the number of miles achieved in a day. The Ford owners often amused themselves by taking apart each other's cars in the hope of locating some obscure new rattle. When all else failed they would have a look under the dashboard at the timer, that mysterious little box of coils with vibrators that you had to adjust. There were many schools of thought about what should be done with a temperamental timer.

"When mine goes wrong," the man from Tennessee said that evening, "I spit in it."

We were to learn as we went along that Henrietta was seldom ready to start after a night in the open, and we developed a regular morning routine. We would get everything packed, put on our coats, sweaters and scarves and climb in. Kit would step on the starter and of course nothing would happen. We would look surprised, prime the engine and try some more. Still no result. Then I would get out, take off my coat, sweater and scarf and turn over the crank. We knew it wouldn't do any good for what Henrietta was holding out for was spinning which neither of us had the strength to do, but, out of the corner of my eye, I could see the men in camp looking our way. I would keep turning and, if necessary, go to the tool box and get out the jack with much rattling. Jacking up the rear wheels was supposed to help but it never did.

Eventually a man would saunter over.

"What's the matter? Won't she start?"

"Oh yes," one of us would say cheerfully, "but she's a little cold."

"Guess she needs spinning."

"That might help . . . ."

157

So he'd spin, and then all the other men in camp would decide he was doing it wrong and come to try it their way. It would develop into a contest and finally, when Henrietta got good and ready, she would give a giggling sound inside her, chuckle awhile, and then settle down to the steady rattle which meant business. I would put on my coat, sweater and scarf and we'd toot off, leaving the perspiring mob congratulating the fellow who finally got the result.

A PLEASURE OF OLD-TIME MOTORING

The famous artist-writer-collector of early Americana, Eric Sloane, reminisces about his experiences driving across the country in a Model A Ford.

Being able to fold the windshield forward and down over the hood, as we could on the Model A, was one of the thrills of old-time motoring, for it let you feel the wind full on your face and enjoy the landscape with your nose. The word "smell" has an unpleasant connotation nowadays, but there was a time when you could really smell the world around you and most times find it enjoyable. Imagine, for example, driving through cooling afternoon air laden with the smell of honeysuckle or of fresh-cut grass, or descending after sunset into cool lowlands where the swamp air is rich with the musk of reeds. When the landscape has that much to offer your nose, it is a pleasure to ride with the windshield pushed down. Even after dark you would still be aware of each kind of field you passed, your nose feeling the presence of sweet, wet air around millponds, the dank wood smell of ancient buildings, or the rich, live smell of barnyard animals around some farm.

TOONERVILLE TROLLEY

Important to the growth of cities in pre-automobile America was the trolley, or streetcar. The heyday of the interurban trolley was celebrated and spoofed by Fontaine Fox, a newspaper cartoonist from Louisville whose "Toonerville Folks" panels attained national syndication in 1915.

Fox's characters were everyday people with comical and endearing idiosyncrasies, often composites of two or more people he knew in real life. "The Toonerville Trolley That Meets All Trains" and its Skipper were inspired by two rundown trolley lines that Fox had traveled on and a friendly old motorman he knew.

ROOSEVELT FIELD, MAY 20, 1927

As 25-year-old Charles A. Lindbergh sat alone, with his bag of five sandwiches, in the cockpit of the "Spirit of St. Louis" on a wet morning in May, listening to his single engine warming up and contemplating the telephone wires at the far end of Roosevelt Field, he carefully weighed the many pros and cons of taking off for Paris. Will the heavily-loaded ship lift off the runway? Will the engine take the long grind across the Atlantic? Will ... But at length he decided that "the wheels will leave the ground, that the wings will rise above the wires, and it is time to start the flight." Here is his own description of the start of the 33½-hour journey that made aviation history.

I buckle my safety belt, pull goggles down over my eyes, turn to the men at the blocks, and nod. Frozen figures leap to action. A yank on the ropes—the wheels are free. I brace myself against the left side of the cockpit, sight along the edge of the runway, and ease the throttle wide open. Now, in seconds, we'll have the answer. Action brings confidence and relief.

But, except for noise and vibration, what little effect the throttle has! The plane creeps heavily forward. Several men are pushing on wing struts to help it start—pushing so hard I'm afraid the struts will buckle. How can I possibly gain flying speed? Why did I ever think that air could carry such a weight?

Why have I placed such reliance on a sheet of paper's curves? What possible connection is there between the intersection of a pencil's lines in San Diego and the ability of this airplane, here, now, to fly?

The *Spirit of St. Louis* feels more like an overloaded truck than an airplane. The tires rut through mud as though they really were on truck wheels. Even the breath of wind is pressing me down. A take-off seems hopeless; but I may as well go on for another hundred feet before giving up. Now that I've started, it's better to make a real attempt. Besides———it's just possible———

Gradually, the speed increases. Maybe the runway's not too soft. Is it long enough? The engine's snarl sounds inadequate and weak, carrying its own note of mechanical frustration. There's none of the spring forward that always before preceded the take-off into air—no lightness of wing, no excess power. The stick wobbles loosely from side to side, and slipstream puts hardly any pressure against rudder. Nothing about my plane has the magic quality of flight. But men begin stumbling off from the wing struts. We're going faster.

A hundred yards of runway passes. The last man drops off the struts. The stick's wobbling changes to lurching motion as ailerons protest unevenness of surface. How long can the landing gear stand such strain? Five thousand pounds crushing down upon it! I keep my eyes fixed on the runway's edge. I must hold the plane straight. One wheel off and the *Spirit of St. Louis* would ground-loop and splinter in the mud. Controls begin to tighten against the pressure of my hand and feet. There's a living quiver in the stick. I have to push hard to hold it forward. Slight movement of the rudder keeps the nose on course. Good signs, but more than a thousand feet have passed. Is there still time, still space?

Pace quickens———turf becomes a blur———the tail skid lifts off ground———I feel the load shifting from wheels to wings. But the runway's slipping by quickly. The halfway mark is just ahead, and I have nothing like flying speed———The engine's turning faster—smoothing out—the propeller's taking better hold—I can tell by the sound. What r.p.m.? But I can't look at instruments—I must hold the runway, not take my eyes from its edge for an instant. An inch off on stick or rudder, and my flight will end.

The halfway mark streaks past---seconds now to decide—close the throttle, or will I get off? The wrong decision means a crash—probably in flames---I pull the stick back firmly, and---The wheels leave the ground. Then I'll get off! The wheels touch again. I ease the stick forward—almost flying speed, and nearly 2000 feet of field ahead---A shallow pool on the runway---water spews up from the tires---A wing drops—lifts as I shove aileron against it—the entire plane trembles from the shock---Off again—right wing low—pull it up---Ease back onto the runway—left rudder—hold to center—must keep straight---Another pool—water drumming on the fabric---The next hop's longer---I could probably stay in air; but I let the wheels touch once more—lightly, a last bow to earth, a gesture of humility before it---Best to have plenty of control with such a load, and control requires speed.

The *Spirit of St. Louis* takes herself off the next time—full flying speed—the controls taut, alive, straining—and still a thousand feet to the web of telephone wires. Now, I have to make it—there's no alternative. It'll be close, but the margin has shifted to my side. I keep the nose down, climbing slowly, each second gaining speed. If the engine can hold out for one more minute---five feet---twenty---forty---wires flash by underneath—twenty feet to spare!

Green grass and bunkers below—a golf links—people looking up. A low, tree-covered hill ahead—I shallow-bank right to avoid it, still grasping the stick tightly as though to steady the plane with my own strength, hardly daring to drop a wing for the turn, hardly daring to push the rudder. The *Spirit of St. Louis* seems balanced on a pin point, as though the slightest movement of controls would cause it to topple over and fall. Five thousand pounds suspended from those little wings—5000 pounds balanced on a blast of air.

IN THE AIR—1936

The following selection comes from a column called "The Bowling Green," which was initiated and conducted by Christopher Morley, and which appeared in the New York EVENING POST and in SATURDAY REVIEW OF LITERATURE. It was one of the best literary columns of the 20's and 30's.

When you know you're going to fly you watch the weather. The best place to get a look at it in our office building is from the washroom window. (That washroom has more influence on literature than you might suppose. There literary editors retire for occasional seclusion, to gaze off over one of Midtown's relatively open spaces, toward the steeps of Radio City, and make up their minds about some book they're reading.) It was a mild soft afternoon. As the bather feels the water with his hand before plunging in, I like to reach out and feel the air before flying. That air (I wished it could realize it) was going to carry considerable responsibility. I reached out and sifted a handful of it. It didn't seem thick enough. But walking through Times Square a few minutes later there was a tepid little breeze which felt more palpable; comfortingly supportive.

At the Air Desk, Penn Station: you study the folder. TWA's little picture of the pilot with a gyroscope inside his head is always comforting. You reflect that, in your own affairs, a little more gyroscopic control would be desirable.

In the limousine en route to Airport: the good old motto on the Main P. O. is an appropriate salute. *Not snow nor rain nor heat nor gloom of night stays these couriers on their appointed rounds.* Herodotus, isn't it? Why wouldn't *The Spirit of Herodotus* be a good name for a plane? Sometimes you almost wish something would stay those chauffeurs a little. On that amazing ramp that runs from Jersey City to Newark they touch 60, in plentiful traffic. The only part of flying that scares one is getting to the airport.

Airport: There she is, great silver Douglas, eagerly nosed up NC13711, Skyliner *City of Chicago.* The 7 and the 11 should take the curse off the 13. (Air passengers are always superstitious.) Weight, please?

Air news reporters always assume that everyone boarding the Sky Chief is on the way to Hollywood on a contract. They are shocked when you let them down by saying you're only going to Columbus.

She turns her silver snoot toward sun. A roaring tryout of motors. Just this one moment I always keep my mind inboard. I try not to think anything heavy, or remember how the Peruvian pelicans used to struggle to get into the air. Those Newark marshes are unpleasantly near. This is the time to be busy with small concerns: fasten belt, accept gum from trim little hostess (did you know that they're not allowed to weigh more than 118, nor to marry within three years), admire one's own little stock of gadgets—air vent, reading lamp, ash tray with little convenient tab for stubbing out cigarette.

Only 25 minutes out and over the Delaware already. On neatly striped roads below are cars creeping along: one passes another, both apparently crawling: this is faintly amusing to watch, probably because you are thinking that they are supposing they are going fast; and to see someone else thinking absolute what you (from taller purview) consider only relative, is always satisfying to the interior gyroscope.—You try not to say to yourself that the cars look "just like ants." But they do, exactly.

5:35 p.m. Pretty little points of light, red and green for port and starboard, brighten the ends of the broad silver wings. Approaching hills of Pennsylvania, Hostess lady (herself a delicious streamline figure) has also brightened herself with rouge, you observe. This is all part of the psychology of air traffic: but to be thoroughly nautical it should be rouge on left cheek and green on right. She is fastening the tray to your chair-arms for supper. Those marvellous cardboard picnic-boxes are the best fun of all: and shrewdly served to divert the mind from the bumpier bits of the Alleghanies. She yaws a bit (the plane, I mean), sways gently (myself I like it: feel of a yacht in a quarterly run of swell). She comes down the aisle (the hostess, I mean) with the big thermos flask, genuflects beside you like a priestess, carefully pours out hot coffee. We're crossing the Susquehanna, 6:05 p.m. Quite a little bump just then, as we skim over a solid chunk of air (it probably bounced up from the capitol at Harrisburg). Hope she won't spill that very hot coffee on her hand. There's a scar above the thumb.

You rummage that luxurious lunch-box (three joints of roast chicken, still warm from the Airport kitchen. Even the food has wings. Looking forward along the aisle you have a humorous vista of passengers gnawing away). Eating, you contemplate nasty parallel ridges of Alleghany, sharp wooded hogbacks fading into dusk. There are still some glints of snow in wrinkles of the hills.

7 p.m.—a sprinkle of lights below. Her great wing sinks softly, softly downward below you as she banks a wide turn. Loveliest of feelings, that slow eiderdown sinking, tilting. She drifts you down through the dark—the gray wing swims sideways and groping, reaching—oh, like a lazy shark in a green aquarium tank—you are coming back, almost with grief, to the heavy bond of earth—a little jolt, a softly rocking run with a few reluctant skips, a roar as the propellors change pitch—you taxi to a brilliant gangway. It's Pittsburgh.

Only about 75 minutes from Pittsburgh to Columbus, but what soft ones. Thinking vaguely of some line of Emily Dickinson's about the bumble bee moving like a train on rails of plush? The little lights click on and off as each passenger turns from reading to study the sky. Clear now, and more stars than one sees on the ground—Orion, for instance, has a lot more accoutrements in his hunting gear. The man in front of me gets out a star-map for March and verifies it.

I wish I'd left space to add that, only two days later, I had the pleasure of accompaning [a] friend . . . on his first flying experience. Columbus to Cleveland in a Condor; then (with one minute for the change) Cleveland to Chicago by Boeing. The first hop was bumpy and [my friend] . . . chewed hard; I was worried for him when a lady up forward went into reverse. But in the smooth Chicago run he relaxed gaily; before long he was asking the hostess's special permission to smoke a cigar; and when he was told that he was dining at 9000 feet he was in an ecstasy. The new moon seemed to be hung just over his right ear, and he was pleased by her shimmer on the round snout of the Pratt & Whitney (where, flying against sunset light, you can just guess the dim haze or halo-circle of the roaring blades).

ASK THAT MAN

This delightful piece by one of our best-loved humorists is taken from THE BENCHLEY ROUND-UP, *a collection of Robert Benchley's most popular essays, as selected by his son, Nathaniel.*

This is written for those men who have wives who are constantly insisting on their asking questions of officials.

For years I was troubled with the following complaint: Just as soon as we started out on a trip of any kind, even if it were only to the corner of the street, Doris began forcing me to ask questions of people. If we weren't quite sure of the way: "Why don't you ask that man? He could tell you." If there was any doubt as to the best place to go to get chocolate ice-cream, she would say, "Why don't you ask that boy in uniform? He would be likely to know."

I can't quite define my aversion to asking questions of strangers. From snatches of family battles which I have heard drifting up from railway stations and street corners, I gather that there are a great many men who share my dislike for it, as well as an equal number of women who, like Doris, believe it to be the solution of most of this world's problems. The man's dread is probably that of making himself appear a pest or ridiculously uninformed. The woman's insistence is based probably on experience which has taught her that anyone, no matter who, knows more about things in general than her husband.

Furthermore, I never know exactly how to begin a request for information. If I preface it with, "I beg your pardon!" the stranger is likely not to hear, especially if he happens to be facing in another direction, for my voice isn't very reliable in crises and sometimes makes no intelligible sound at all until I have been talking for fully a minute. Often I say, "I beg your pardon!" and he turns quickly and says, "What did you say?" Then I have to repeat, "I beg your pardon!" and he asks, quite naturally, "What for?" Then I am stuck. Here I am, begging a perfect stranger's pardon, and for no apparent reason under the sun. The wonder is that I am not knocked down oftener.

It was to avoid going through life under this pressure that I evolved the little scheme detailed herewith. It cost me several thousand dollars, but Doris is through with asking questions of outsiders.

We had started on a little trip to Boston. I could have found out where the Boston train was in a few minutes had I been left to myself. But Doris never relies on the signs. Someone must be asked, too, just to make sure. Confronted once by a buckboard literally swathed in banners which screamed in red letters, "This bus goes to the State Fair Grounds," I had to go up to the driver (who had on his cap a flag reading "To the State Fair Grounds") and ask him if this bus surely went to the State Fair Grounds. He didn't even answer me.

So when Doris said, "Go and ask that man where the Boston train leaves from," I gritted my teeth and decided that the time had come. Simulating conversation with him, I really asked him nothing, and returned to Doris, saying, "Come on. He says it goes from Track 10."

Eight months later we returned home. The train that left on Track 10 was the Chicago Limited, which I had taken deliberately. In Chicago I again falsified what "the man" told me, and instead of getting on the train back to New York we went to Little Rock, Arkansas. Every time I had to ask where the best hotel was, I made up information which brought us out into the suburbs, cold and hungry. Many nights we spent wandering through the fields looking for some place that never existed, or else in the worst hotel in town acting on what I said was the advice of "that kind-looking man in uniform."

From Arkansas, we went into Mexico, and once, guided by what I told her had been the directions given me by the man at the news-stand in Vera Cruz, we made a sally into the swamps of Central America, or whatever that first republic is on the way south. After that, Doris began to lose faith in what strange men could tell us. One day, at a little station in Mavicos, I said, "Wait a minute, till I ask that man what is the best way to get back into America," and she said sobbing, "Don't ask anybody. Just do what you think is best." Then I knew that the fight was over. In ten days I had her limp form back in New York and from that day to this she hasn't once suggested that I ask questions of a stranger.

The funny part of it is, I constantly find myself asking them. I guess the humiliation came in being told to ask.

SUPERJETS FOR THE AIRLANES

Early plane travel was marked by cramped seating, frequent refueling stops, and hazardous juggling acts during meal-times aloft. Then along came the jets, which could carry twice as many people, twice as fast, in a virtually silk-smooth ride. Finally, the big jets arrived—the 747, the DC-10 and the L-1011—again carrying more people faster and in greater comfort.

These superjets are wide-bodied and roomy. To dramatize spaciousness in television advertising, one airline filmed the Harlem Globetrotters tossing basketballs around in a 747, then brought the Seattle Symphony Orchestra into a cabin for a televised concert. The 747 cabin is 65 feet longer than the distance flown by Orville Wright in his first successful flight in 1903.

A cat named Garfunkel set some sort of record as a superjet stowaway. He boarded at Oshkosh, Wisconsin, en route to Anchorage, Alaska. Somewhere along the way, he slipped out of his homemade cage and into the bowels of the 747 to expend a few of his nine lives. He flew between North America and the Orient for three weeks, and was finally discovered when the plane returned to the factory for modifications. There a mechanic saw him in his hiding place between the insulation blanket and the wall of the airliner. A trap was baited with catfood and he was retrieved unharmed but famished. After recuperating in an animal hospital, Garfunkel completed his trip to Anchorage, first class.

The late Charles A. Lindbergh, first person to fly solo across the Atlantic, discovered that fame can be fleeting when he traveled the same route 46 years later in a 747. After the plane took off from New York, the captain announced, "Ladies and gentlemen, we have the pleasure and honor to number Mr. Charles Lindbergh among our passengers." Mr. Lindbergh stood up and nodded pleasantly. Settling himself again, he had a little difficulty with the seat-belt. A young stewardess came to help him and asked, "Is this your first crossing, Mr. Lindbergh?"

— Robert N. McCready

BUCK ROGERS

To a kid in the 1930's, and indeed many adults, the romance of new adventures in travel might have gone unnoticed had it not been for the science fiction comic strip "Buck Rogers," written by Philip Nowlan and drawn by Dick Calkins. The automobile was comfortably here to stay, the airplane could only become bigger and faster, but the incredible voyage of Buck Rogers into the 25th century offered space rockets and interplanetary expeditions.

HEADQUARTERS
BUCK ROGERS SOLAR SCOUTS
Earth Division

Official Enlistment Papers

Pursuant to orders from SCOUT PATROL UNIT, G. H. Q. NIAGARA, all applicants for enrollment in the BUCK ROGERS INTERPLANETARY SOLAR SCOUTS are requested to fill out this ENLISTMENT BLANK and return it to the headquarters immediately.

DATA REQUIRED

1. NAME
2. Age
3. Height
4. Weight
5. Color of Eyes
6. Color of Hair

7. School Grade
8. Favorite Sports
9. Previous Rocket Ship experience, if any
10. Favorite Newspaper Adventure Strip

THE MISSION

Journeys by Americans gained a new dimension on February 20, 1962, when Lt. Col. John H. Glenn, Jr., became the first American in orbit when he circled the earth three times in the Mercury capsule Friendship 7. What did Florida look like as Glenn watched it recede at a rate of nearly five miles per second? How did a sunset appear (Glenn saw four sunsets in one day)? Were there any strange, new sights to be encountered? In the book WE SEVEN *, written by the astronauts themselves, John Glenn describes the view from a space capsule.*

About a minute and a half before lift-off, I did a few quick exercises to make sure that my body was toned and ready for the launch. The aeromed people asked for one final blood-pressure check before lift-off. They had been asking for this all through the count, and pushed a button which started the recording instrument and I pumped up the bulb, took the blood-pressure reading automatically from a cuff on my left arm and sent it along by telemetry to the Control Center. Then, I put my left hand on the abort handle, as procedure requires. At T minus 35 seconds, a special countdown started for dropping the umbilical cord which had been providing external power and cooling for the capsule up until now. This was the last physical link between the capsule and the ground, and I watched through the periscope as the umbilical fell away and I heard it fall with a loud plop. The periscope retracted automatically, and this shut off my view from that direction. The land lines to the blockhouse and Control Center were cut off now and we communicated from now on only by radio. I could detect a tone of excitement in the voices in my headset, and as the countdown we had practiced so often ran down for this final time, I shared the feeling. At T minus 18 seconds there was a planned momentary hold of two or three seconds while the automatic engine starter was switched on. I did not hear it at the time, but just as the engine sequence started and he knew this was it, Scott spoke into his microphone in the blockhouse. "Godspeed, John Glenn," he said. I heard it later on a recording of the transmissions; it was a very impressive moment. No one would push any more buttons or take any further positive action now—except to stop the show at the last second in case of an emergency. Then Al Shepard's voice gave me the final 10 seconds of the count. He reached zero and the engines started.

I could feel the engines light off as the capsule vibrated from their ignition, and I could hear a faint roar inside the capsule. The booster stood fast on the pad for two or three seconds while the engines built up to their proper thrust. Then the big hold-down clamps dropped away and I could feel us start to go. I had always thought from watching Atlas launches that it would seem slow and a little sluggish, like an elevator rising. I was wrong; it was not like that at all. It was a solid and exhilarating surge of up and away. Al Shepard received a signal that I was lifting off and confirmed it for me over the radio. The capsule clock started right on time and I reported this.

"The clock is operating," I said. "We're under way."

. . .

This was it. We were 100 miles up and going at a velocity of 25,730 feet per second. I went weightless as the G forces dropped from 6 to zero; it was a very pleasant sensation. The periscope extended, and the capsule began to turn around automatically to orbital attitude—blunt end forward—which it would hold throughout the three orbits. The automatic system accomplished this maneuver by activating the nozzles which then turned the capsule. Now, for the first time, I could look out the window and see back along the flight path. I could not help exclaiming over the radio about what I saw. "Oh," I said, "that view is tremendous!" It really was. I could see for hundreds of miles in every direction—the sun on white clouds, patches of blue water beneath and great chunks of Florida and the south-eastern U.S.

. . .

Since I was facing backwards, everything came out from underneath me, similar to the way things look when you ride backwards in a car, and it seemed to move more rapidly than I had thought it would. The sense of speed was similar to what you normally experience in a jet airliner at about 30,000 feet when you are looking down on a cloud bank at low altitudes. I think our training devices had been a little inadequate on this score; they had given us less sensation of motion and speed than I could feel in actual flight. Just before I finished crossing the Atlantic, I had my last glimpses of the Atlas. It was still in orbit, about two miles behind me and a mile beneath me. It was bright enough so that I could see it even against the bright background of the earth.

I saw the Canary Islands through the periscope and then saw them through the window. They were partially hidden by clouds. While I was reporting in by radio to the Canary Island tracking station I had my first glimpse of the coast of Africa. The Atlas Mountains were clearly visible through the window. In-land, I could see huge dust storms blowing across the desert, as well as clouds of smoke from brush fires raging along the edge of the desert. One of the things that surprised me most about the flight was the percentage of the earth which was covered by clouds. They were nearly solid over Central Africa and extended out over most of the Indian Ocean and clear across the Pacific. I could not establish the exact altitude of all of the various layers, but I could easily determine where one layer ended and another layer began by the shadows, and I believe that with better optical instruments we can contribute a good deal to the art of weather forecasting from this orbital altitude.

. . .

We had hoped to make some observations of the moon and stars from orbital altitude during the three 40-minute nights

172

which I would experience on the flight, in order to determine how visible the horizon would be at night and how useful it might be for maintaining the capsule's attitude. This meant that I had to be prepared for night vision—or "dark adapted"—well before night came. I placed red covers over the lights in the cockpit and turned off the special photo-lights which helped us make pictures of my reactions during the flight. I turned on the tiny bulbs which we had had installed at the ends of the index and middle fingers on each glove. These served as miniature flashlights and were very useful. I also tried to install the special eyepatch which had been molded to fit the left side of my face. The patch did not work very well, however. My face was moist and the special tape we had brought along failed to keep the patch in place.

I witnessed my first sunset over the Indian Ocean, and it was a beautiful display of vivid colors. The sun is perfectly round and it gives off an intense, clear light which is more bluish-white than yellow, and which reminded me in color and intensity of the huge arc lights we used at the Cape. It was so bright that I had to use filters to look directly at it. Then, just as the sun starts to sink into the bright horizon, it seems to flatten out a little. As the sun gets lower and lower, a black shadow moves across the earth until the entire surface that you can see is dark except for the bright band of light along the horizon. At the beginning, this band is almost white in color. But as the sun sinks deeper the bottom layer of light turns to bright orange. The next layers are red, then purple, then light blue, then darker blue and finally the blackness of space. They are all brilliant colors, more brilliant than in a rainbow, and the band extends out about 60 degrees on either side of the sun. It is a fabulous display. I watched the first sunset through an instrument we call a photometer, which has a polarizing filter mounted on the front of it so you can look directly at the sun without hurting your eyes. I discovered later that it was possible to look directly at the sun without the photometer, just by squinting my eyes, the same as we have always done from here on the surface of the earth. We had thought that perhaps it would be too bright for that above the atmosphere.

I saw a total of four sunsets before the day was over—three during the flight and a final one after I had landed and been picked up by the destroyer. Each time I saw it set, the sun was slightly to my left, and I turned the spacecraft around a little on its yaw axis to get a better view. One thing that interested me was the length of the twilight. The brilliant band of light along the horizon was visible for up to five minutes after the sun went down, which is a long time considering the fact that I was moving away from the sunset and watching it occur at eighteen times the speed at which we normally watch sunsets from down here on earth.

Then the earth was dark; looking down at it was like gazing into a black pit. It was bright again, however, as soon as the moon came up. The moon was almost full. The clouds below showed up clearly in the moonlight, and I was able to estimate my angle of drift by looking down at the formations far below me.

I was able to see the horizon at night, and this enabled me to correct the attitude of my spacecraft against the horizontal plane of the earth below. I noticed an unexpected effect along the horizon on the nightside. There seemed to be a layer of haze about 2 degrees thick which hung about 6 to 8 degrees above the real horizon and lay parallel to it. I first noticed this phenomenon over the Indian Ocean as I was watching the stars set. They became dim for a few seconds as they approached the horizon and then they brightened again before they finally went out of sight. I looked carefully, and there seemed to be a definite band of some kind where they dimmed. It was not white like the moonlit clouds, but more tan or buff in color. And it did not have a definite configuration. The only real sign that a layer of some kind was there was that the stars dimmed as they passed through this area and then brightened again. The same phenomenon occurred on all three orbits, and it was most noticeable when the moon was up.

I had thought that I might be able to see more stars than I did. I was prepared to study the various constellations and group-ings and count the number of stars in each one to see if I could spot any that we do not normally see clearly from beneath the atmosphere. I did see a whole sky full of stars, and it was a beautiful sight. The effect was much the same as you would have if you went out into a desert on a clear night and looked up. It was not much more than that, however. Laboratory tests of the window made before the flight were correct. The heavy glass in the window provided about the same attenuation that the atmosphere does, and though I saw the stars clearly—and they did not twinkle—I saw about the same number as you would on a clear night from earth. We will probably have to have a new kind of window before we can do much better. I did see a few stars during the day, shining against the black sky. But they were far more clear at night. The stars that I saw at night were of some help in delineating the horizon so I could control the attitude of the capsule. The constellations of Orion and the Pleiades were especially bright, and on one pass over the Indian Ocean I focused on Orion through the center of the window and used it as my only reference for maintaining attitude. All in all, a night in space is a beautiful sight. You see the moon shining bright on the clouds far below you and fields of stars silhouetting the horizon for hundreds of miles in each direction. Just like the sun, the moon and the stars declined and finally set at a speed eighteen times faster from my fast-moving, orbital vantage point than they do for us here on earth.

I saw my first and only signs of man-made light as I came over Australia on my first pass. Looking through the window, I could see several great patches of brightness down below. Gordon Cooper, who was on duty as the Cap Com at the tracking station in Muchea, Australia, had alerted me to look off to the right. He knew that the citizens of Perth and several other cities and towns along the coast had turned on all of the lights they had as a greeting, and when I spotted them I asked him to thank everyone for being so thoughtful.

. . .

The strangest sight of the entire flight came a few seconds later. I was watching the sunrise, which suddenly filled the scope with a brilliant red, and had put a filter onto the scope to cut down the glare. Then I glanced out of the window and looked back towards the dark western horizon. It was a startling sight. All around me, as far as I could see, were thousands and thousands of small, luminous particles. I thought for a minute that I must have drifted upside down and was looking up at a new field of stars. I checked my instruments to make sure that I was rightside up. Then I looked again. I was in contact with the

175

Canton Island tracking station at the time, and I tried to tell the Cap Com there what it was like.

"This is Friendship Seven," I began. "I'll try to describe what I'm in here. I am in a big mass of very small particles that are brilliantly lit up like they're luminescent. I never saw anything like it. They're coming by the capsule, and they look like little stars. A whole shower of them coming by. They swirl around the capsule and go in front of the window and they're all brilliantly lighted. They probably average seven or eight feet apart, but I can see them all down below me, also."

The Canton Island Cap Com came on the air and asked if I could hear any impact between the particles and the capsule.

"Negative," I reported. "They're very slow; they're not going away from me more than maybe three or four miles per hour. They're going at the same speed I am approximately. They're only very slightly under my speed. They do have a different motion, though, from me because they swirl around the capsule and then depart back the way I am looking."

The particles seemed to disappear in the glare as soon as the sun came up. But I saw them again under the same conditions on the next orbit. This time, although I was having a few troubles with the capsule, I turned it around 180 degrees in order to look at the particles from another direction. I wanted to see if perhaps they were emanating from the capsule itself. They did not appear to be, however. They were not centered around the capsule but were stretched out as far as I could see. I saw fewer of them this time, because I was looking against the sun. But some of them still came drifting towards me, just as they had done when I first saw them. They were yellowish green in color, and they appeared to vary in size from a pinhead to perhaps three-eighths of an inch. They had the same color, luminous quality and approximate intensity of light as fireflies, and the sensation as I slowly rode through them was like walking backwards through a pasture where someone had waved a wand and made all of the fireflies stop right where they were and glow steadily.

I saw the particles once more on the third orbit, again just as the first rays of the sun appeared over the horizon. They stayed in sight for about four minutes, some of them turning dark as they went into the shadow of the capsule, others swirling up

176

past the window and changing direction as I moved through them. It was a fascinating spectacle, and though various scientists have assumed since that the particles were undoubtedly emanating from the capsule itself, I found this hard to believe. I thought at first that they might be a layer of tiny needles that the Air Force had sent into space on a communications experiment and had then lost. But needles would not have been luminescent—nor was I at the proper altitude. I also thought that they might be tiny snowflakes formed by the condensation of water vapor from the control nozzles. I intentionally blipped the thrusters to see if they gave off particles. They gave off steam, but no particles that I could see. The particles were a mystery at the time, and they have remained one as far as I'm concerned. Our staff psychiatrist, Dr. George Ruff, heard me describe them at one of the debriefings after the flight, and he had only one question: "What did they say, John?" I guess they were as speechless as I was.

. . .

I could look down and see the entire state of Florida and clear back to the delta of the Mississippi River around New Orleans. This was the best view I had had of the U.S. There was a cloud deck to the north, but I could see as far north as North Carolina. To the south I spotted islands east of Cuba. I looked out over the Atlantic to check the recovery area where I would be landing the next time around. There were a few scattered clouds but no sign of a major weather system. The sea seemed to be placid, though it was so far below me I could not really tell. I had noticed the wake of a ship on a previous pass over the Atlantic, and I assumed it might have been one of the three aircraft carriers, standing by waiting to launch helicopters to pick me up.

. . .

I turned the capsule to the left a little on the yaw axis as I crossed the Atlantic in order to get a better view of my third sunset of the day. I described the sight to the Atlantic Ocean tracking ship and said that I could see a very orange band along the horizon, then a lighter yellow on top of that, followed by a very deep blue, a very light blue and then the black sky. I also reported that it was not too easy to see anything through the window when I was looking towards the sun. It appeared, I said, as if "we might have smashed some bugs on the way up off the pad. Looks like blood on the outside of the window." There was

177

no attendant around to wash this windshield.

As I passed the tip of Africa and started over the Indian Ocean I could see a huge storm front stretching out beneath me as far as I could see. It was dark now, and the ocean itself was covered with a thick layer of clouds. But I could see bright flashes of lightning inside the clouds. The weather people had wondered whether I would be able to see lightning from such a high altitude. The flashes showed up brilliantly, like flashbulbs being popped off behind a white sheet. Each flash lit up an entire bank of clouds.

. . .

I was descending now at the rate of 42 feet per second and had 5 minutes and 10 seconds left before impact. I contacted the destroyer *Noa*, which had the code name of "Steelhead," and told the skipper that my condition was good but that it was a little hot inside the capsule. He informed me that he had picked up on his radar the chaff which the main chute had kicked out and that he was heading in my direction. He estimated that it would take him about an hour to get on station.

I started to run down the checklist of landing procedures. I unfastened from my pants leg the plug which connected the biomedical sensors. I removed the blood-pressure equipment from the suit, loosened the chest strap and got it free, unhooked the respiration sensor from my lip mike and stuffed it inside my suit, disconnected the oxygen exhaust hose from the helmet and unstowed the survival pack that I had to the left of my couch and kept it handy in case of an emergency. Al Shepard got on the radio at this point to make sure that my landing-bag light was on green so that it would deploy and take up the shock of landing.

"That's affirmative," I said. "Landing bag is on green."

Then Al came on again to recommend that I remain in the capsule unless I had "an overriding reason for getting out." He knew that the destroyer was only about 6 miles from where I would land and that instead of using helicopters to pick me up as we had planned, I would have to be hoisted aboard by the destroyer. It would be simpler in this case if I stayed shut up inside so we would not take any chance on losing the capsule. We had rehearsed this method of recovery as well as the helicopter method, so I was prepared for either one and I rogered for his message. I kept up a running account now of my approach to the water so that everyone on the network would know my status.

"Friendship Seven," I said, 48 seconds before I hit. "Ready for impact; almost down."

Fifteen seconds later: "Friendship Seven. Getting close. Standing by."

Twenty seconds later: "Here we go."

Ten seconds after that: "Friendship Seven. Impact. Rescue Aids is manual."

I pushed the button which started the flashing light on top of the capsule and the automatic radio signals which would help the recovery force home in on my position.

The capsule hit the ocean with a good solid bump, and went far enough under water to submerge both the periscope and the window. I could hear gurgling sounds almost immediately. After it listed over to the right and then to the left, the capsule righted itself and I could find no traces of any leaks. I undid the seat strap now and the shoulder harness, disconnected my helmet and put up my neck dam so I could not get water inside my suit if I had to get into the ocean. I was sweating profusely and was very uncomfortable. I kept the suit fans going, but they did not help much. The snorkels in the capsule wall were pumping in outside air, but it was extremely humid outside and this did not help to cool me off one bit, either. I thought about removing the lid of the capsule and climbing on out. But I decided against it. I knew that any body movement would only generate more heat and make me even warmer. The thing to do was sit tight, stay motionless and try to keep as cool as possible.

"Steelhead" kept up a running commentary on how she was doing. First, she was 4 minutes away, then she slowed down and was 3 minutes away; then her engines were stopped and she was coming alongside. The capsule window was so clogged now with both resin and sea water that I could not see her. Strangely enough, however, the capsule bobbed around in the water until the periscope was pointing directly at the destroyer, and it kept her in view from then on. I could read her number—841—and I could see so many sailors in white uniforms standing on the deck that I asked the captain if he had anybody down below running the ship. He assured me he did. Then he drifted alongside very slowly until we gently bumped into each other.

Two sailors reached over with a shepherd's hook to snag the capsule, and moments later we were on deck. I started to crawl through the top to avoid blowing the side hatch and jiggling the instruments inside the capsule. I was still so uncomfortably hot, however, that I decided there was no point in going out the hard way. After warning the deck crew to stand clear, and receiving clearance that all of the men were out of the way, I hit the handle which blew the hatch. I got my only wound of the day doing it—two skinned knuckles on my right hand where the plunger snapped back into place after I reached back to hit it. Then I climbed out on deck. I was back with people again.

"WHAT A BEAUTIFUL VIEW!"

The first American to experience the tremendous variety of color, land masses and cloud cover to be seen from space was Alan Shepard. He made the initial U.S. manned space flight, from Cape Canaveral, Florida, on May 5, 1961. It was not an orbital flight, but the Redstone rocket carried Shepard more than a hundred miles above the earth.

He had studied special maps which showed him the prospective view, but he was not prepared for its astounding magnificence. Shepard could see all the way from the Florida Keys north to cloud-covered Cape Hatteras and from the Bahama Islands west to Tampa Bay and Pensacola. The brilliantly clear, sharply varied colors around the ocean reefs and islands particularly fascinated him. At his peak of 115 miles above the earth, he witnessed a panorama of 1600 miles.

How did Alan Shepard react to this first sight of America from space? Just like any tourist seeing the Grand Canyon or Niagara Falls for the first time! His report back to his earth-bound associates was simply, "What a beautiful view!"

—Robert N. McCready

"THE EAGLE HAS LANDED"

On July 20, 1969, American astronauts circled the moon 13 times, preparing for the climax of the most dramatic story of our era. John Noble Wilford, aerospace reporter for the New York Times, noted in his book WE REACH THE MOON *that "After centuries of dreams and prophecies, a decade of preparations, and four days of flight, the moment had come." Everything up to then was really only warm-up for the encounter with the unknown on the lunar surface. Neil A. Armstrong and Edwin E. Aldrin, Jr., were in the Eagle, their landing vehicle, about 10 miles above the moon, ready for the final descent.*

Finally, Armstrong found a spot he liked. He eased the Lunar Module down slowly until a blue light on the cockpit flashed to indicate that the five-foot-long probes, like curb feelers, on three of the legs had touched the surface.

"Contact light," Armstrong radioed.

He pressed a button marked "Stop" and reported, "Okay, engine stop."

There were a few more cryptic messages of functions performed. Then Charles M. Duke, the capsule communicator at Mission Control, radioed to the two astronauts, "We copy you down, Eagle."

Then, the historic words: "Houston, Tranquility Base here. The Eagle has landed." It was 4:17 P.M., E.D.T. The module was at an angle of only about 4½ degrees. The angle could have been more than 30 degrees without tipping the vehicle over.

"Roger, Tranquility," ground control replied. "We copy you on the ground. You got a bunch of guys about to turn blue. We are breathing again. Thanks a lot."

Although Armstrong is known as a man of few words, his heartbeats told of his excitement upon leading man's first landing on the moon. At the time of the descent rocket ignition, his heartbeat rate registered 110 a minute—77 is normal for him—and it shot up to 156 at touchdown.

At 10:56 P.M., E.D.T., on July 20, 1969, Neil A. Armstrong stepped into history. From the bottom rung of the ladder leading down from Apollo 11's landing craft, he reached out his booted left foot and planted the first human footprint on the moon.

Then he uttered the long-awaited words that are sure to be immortalized: "That's one small step for man, one giant leap for mankind."

There it was, man meeting moon, his first direct contact with another celestial body. For explorers, it was the realization of centuries of dreams. For scientists, it meant an unprecedented opportunity for possible clues to the origin and nature of both the moon and the earth.

Appropriately, Armstrong was able to share the triumphal moment with mankind. As he descended the ladder, he pulled a lanyard that released a fold-down equipment compartment that deployed a television camera. Thus, through the miracle of modern communications, hundreds of millions of people on earth—probably the largest audience ever—witnessed the astronaut's memorable step via TV and heard his words via radio. It required just 1.3 seconds, the time it takes for radio waves to travel the 238,000 miles between moon and earth, for Armstrong's image to appear on home screens. This gave viewers a feeling of "I was there" when history was made.

What was the new environment like, this remote space frontier suddenly invaded by man? Looking through the windows of the landing craft, the astronauts saw a bleak but strangely beautiful world. It was just before dawn over the Sea of Tranquility, with the sun low over the eastern horizon behind them. The chill of the long lunar night still clung to the boulders, craters and hills before them.

"Magnificent desolation," was the phrase Aldrin used in describing the view. He said that he could see "literally thousands of small craters." But most of all he was impressed initially by the "variety of shapes, angularities, granularities" of the rocks and soil around Tranquility Base.

At one point, Buzz Aldrin radioed this impression of the general area in which they touched down:

"[There is a] level plain cratered with a fairly large number of craters of the 5- to 50-foot variety. And some ridges, small, 20 to 30 feet high, I would guess. And literally thousands of little one- and two-foot craters around the area. We see some angular blocks out several hundred feet in front of us that are probably two feet in size and have angular edges. There is a hill in view just about on the ground track ahead of us. Difficult to estimate, but might be half a mile or a mile. . . .

"I'd say the color of the local surface is very comparable to that we observed from orbit at this sun angle—about 10 degrees sun angle or that nature. It's pretty much without color. It's gray and it's very white as you look into the zero phase line. And it's considerably darker gray, more like an ashen gray, as you look out 90 degrees to the sun. Some of the surface rocks in close here that have been fractured or disturbed by the rocket engine plume are coated with this light gray on the outside. But where they've been broken, they display a dark, very dark, gray interior and it looks like it could be country basalt."

When Armstrong reached the bottom of the Lunar Module's ladder, he found that the moon was indeed not made of green cheese. Observing that "the LM foot pads are only depressed in the surface about one or two inches," he said: "The surface is fine and powdery. I can pick it up loosely with my toe. It does adhere in fine layers like powdered charcoal to the sole and sides of my boots. I only go in a small fraction of an inch, maybe an eighth of an inch. But I can see the footprints of my boots and the treads in the fine, sandy particles."

Then, while the excited audience watched those first few moments in awe, Armstrong tentatively tested the moon's environment and found it relatively receptive. He found that he could move about easily in his bulky white spacesuit and heavy backpack while under the influence of lunar gravity, which makes everything weigh only one-sixth of what it weighs on earth.

After 19 minutes, Armstrong was joined outside the landing craft by Aldrin, who had been preparing and handing down equipment for the two hours of probing and experimenting. The excitement of the moment notwithstanding, Aldrin did not overlook the little necessities. As he emerged through the hatch and started down the ladder, he said, "I want to back up and partially close the hatch, making sure not to lock it on my way out."

"Good thought," Armstrong agreed.

"That's our home for the next couple of hours," Aldrin added. "We want to take good care of it."

Then, as Aldrin started his first testing of the surface, Armstrong commented at one point: "Isn't this fun?"

"Right in this area I don't think there's much fine powder," Aldrin noted. "It's hard to tell whether it's a clod or a rock."

"You can pick it up," Armstrong pointed out.

"And it bounces," was Aldrin's reply.

They immediately set up another TV camera away from the craft to give the people on earth a broader look at the Sea of Tranquility landscape. What was seen during a panoramic camera sweep conformed pretty much with photographs previously transmitted by unmanned satellites: a bleak, empty, almost flat, crater-pocked, undulating surface devoid, of course, of vegetation. Yet, Armstrong described the landscape as having "a stark beauty all its own."

"It's like much of the high desert of the United States," he said. "It's different but it's very pretty out here."

One of the first things the astronauts did to embellish that forbidding and monotonous landscape was to plant their three-foot-by-five-foot American flag. It was stiffened with thin wire so as to appear to be flying on the windless lunar surface.

184

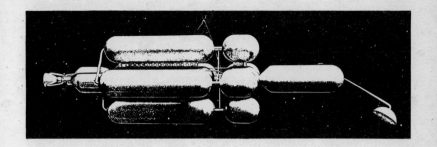

INTERPLANETARY MAN

Where will the future journeys of Americans lead? The drama of earth exploration and settlement is nearly concluded. The new frontiers lie elsewhere, perhaps underseas or in the limitless skies. Arthur C. Clarke, scientist and science-fiction writer, sees some real challenges in interplanetary travel. In an epilogue to the book, FIRST ON THE MOON, *he says, "We must face the possibility–even the probability–that all our history on this world is but prelude to a far more complex future on an infinitely wider stage."*

All our ideas about travel beyond the earth are based upon rocket technology, and indeed we have no other means of propulsion in the vacuum of space. (Even the various nuclear and electric thrusters still depend upon the same principle of reaction or recoil.) However, it may well be that the rocket's history will parallel that of the balloon—which lifted mankind into a new element, but was eventually superseded.

A Saturn liftoff is the most magnificent spectacle yet contrived by man; yet there must be better ways of achieving the same result, more compatible with nervous old ladies visiting their grandchildren on the moon, as well as with the peace and quiet of the countryside. The history of technology teaches us that the right tool always arrives at the right moment; witness how the transistor was ready when the Space Age dawned.

It may be a pure coincidence, but it seems slightly uncanny that success in the long search for gravitational waves was announced only a month before the first landing on the moon—by Dr. Weber of the University of Maryland. The old dream of controlling gravity may be a complete delusion—or it may foreshadow a basic industry of the twenty-first century. Anyone who is unwilling to admit this possibility should remember that when Hertz demonstrated the existence of electromagnetic waves in 1886, he saw no practical use for them. Now there is no man alive who is not affected by the radio networks that enmesh the globe—and are already stretching out to the planets. Perhaps the cycle is beginning again, and may lead to feats of space engineering as incredible to us as television would have been to the Victorians.

Even if such scientific breakthroughs do not happen (which is perhaps the most unlikely of all possibilities!) the entire solar system will become accessible to us during the coming century. Voyage times first measured in years will shrink to months, then to weeks, as nuclear propulsion systems become more efficient. On this planet, the evolution from the sailing ship to the intercontinental jet took three thousand years; the parallel evolution in space may take only a hundred.

And given the solar system—what will we do with it? At the very least, we will establish scientific bases on the more stable and hospitable bodies—such as Mars, Mercury, and the major satellites. Of these, the most important may be Titan, the giant moon of Saturn, which is almost as large as Mercury. However, it may not be unique as a source of methane (and hence hydrogen) for our nuclear rockets. Two of Jupiter's satellites, Ganymede and Callisto, are of about the same size as Titan, and may also serve as bases for the exploration of the outer planets.

Exploring the twenty-nine known (and probably many undiscovered) moons of the four great worlds Jupiter, Saturn, Uranus and Neptune is a task which may take generations; today, it is quite impossible to predict how rewarding, or otherwise, it will be. But exploring the giant planets themselves will be immeasurably more difficult; indeed, it may never be attempted by men, only by instruments. Even if the so-called "gas giants" possess solid surfaces, they may be so far down in their turbulent atmospheres that the pressures may be more crushing than in our deepest oceans. A spaceship capable of landing on (in?) Jupiter would have to be far stronger than any bathyscaphe designed to sound the Pacific trenches, and would have to be powered by energy sources completely beyond any technology we know today. And as an additional minor drawback, the intrepid crew would have to operate in a gravitational field that gave them two-and-a-half times their normal weight.

It would be rash to state that such feats will never be attempted, but more within the range of foreseeable engineering would be the exploration, by what have been called "buoyant stations" (i.e., balloons) of the atmospheres of the giant planets. Combination airship-spaceships, drifting or actively cruising at altitudes where the pressure was not impossibly high, may one day serve us as mobile manned bases on these strange worlds. From such floating platforms, we may send instruments, and beams of radiation, into the inaccessible depths thousands of miles below.

A lighter-than-"air" vehicle for the Jovian atmosphere poses some fascinating technical problems. Jupiter's atmosphere is mostly hydrogen—and as this is the lightest of all gases, what can we possibly put in our balloons so that they will float in such a medium? The answer can only be hydrogen itself—but *heated*. The recent surprising revival of hot-air ballooning as a sport may have important repercussions, half a century from now. It is quite conceivable that some youngster, soaring in today's skies, may be learning skills he will apply in wildly different surroundings, where the horizon is three times further away than on earth. . . .

We may also explore Venus by balloon long before we land on its dully glowing surface—probably first starting at the poles. Venus, unlike the earth, has its spin-axis almost at right angles to its orbit; having no axial tilt, it consequently has no seasons. The polar regions of the planet must therefore be, permanently, hundreds of degrees colder than the lower latitudes. If there are mountains here, water might exist on them—and some wildly optimistic scientists have even suggested the possibility of ice, which could reopen the whole question of Hesperian life.

However, it seems far more probable that any life on Venus (as on the moon) will be imported from earth. The astronomer-biologist Carl Sagan has suggested "seeding" the cloud layers with specially developed microorganisms, which could float in the turbulent upper atmosphere and feed on the immense quantities of carbon dioxide present. While doing this, they would release oxygen, and as their numbers multiplied there would be an ever-accelerating transformation of the atmosphere. In a relatively short time (perhaps centuries, perhaps even decades) the process which took geological ages on earth would have progressed far enough to make Venus hospitable to men.

Similar suggestions have been made regarding Mars, which may also possess vast quantities of oxygen locked up in its surface rocks. The material of the reddish Martian "deserts" may be iron oxide, and bacteria exist which can release its oxygen and leave the iron. This, in fact, is precisely how some of the great terrestrial iron deposits were formed. The bacteria involved have already had an immense economic impact on our own planet; one day we may set them to work again on other worlds.

These suggestions are by no means the most ambitious that have been put forward by reputable scientists. As early as 1948, the famous California Institute of Technology astronomer Fritz Zwicky—who was then heavily involved in the establishment of the American rocket industry—startled his colleagues by proposing the *reconstruction of the solar system*. He predicted that the time would come when man's increasing powers over his environment would allow him, literally, to move worlds, and thus to place the planets in orbits that would give them more favorable climates.

Even more mind-boggling ideas have been discussed by the British mathematician Freeman Dyson. He has argued that no intelligent species would tolerate indefinitely the fact that more than 99.9999999% of its sun's radiation is lost in space, and only a few billionths are intercepted by the planets. As the power requirements of a civilization increased, it might be necessary to dismantle a few planets and shield the sun completely with energy-absorbing screens.

This raises another question, first discussed by Tsiolkovsky during the 1920's in his pioneering studies of astronautics. *Do we really need planets?* When we have solved the purely technical problems of sustaining life in space, why should we continue to tolerate the perpetual drag of gravity, which cripples and sometimes kills us, and perhaps shortens our lives? The blissful weightlessness of free fall has now been experienced by a handful of astronauts—but has also been glimpsed by millions of skin-divers. It has its inconveniences, but these are easy to overcome. We evolved in the weightless environment of the sea; when we get into space, we may discover that this is where we really belong....

Forty years ago, in an astonishing and recently reprinted book *The World, the Flesh and the Devil,* the British physicist J.D. Bernal suggested that eventually most of mankind would live in spherical space cities a few miles in diameter, moving in independent orbits around the sun. If this is correct, it is possible that far more people will live *off* the earth than the approximately one hundred billion who have lived on it since the dawn of time.

We must face the possibility—even the probability—that all our history on this world is but prelude to a far more complex future on an infinitely wider stage. On and among the planets we may see the founding of new societies, new cultures—perhaps even new species, as our descendants naturally or artificially adapt to alien environments.

There are some who may recoil in horror from these vertiginous glimpses of a cosmic future, or may feel that even to discuss them diverts attention from the immediate and desperate problems of our present age. That danger indeed exists; here—and only here—the tired old charge of "escapism" may sometimes be made against those whose eyes are fixed upon the stars. Yet to let our minds wander from time to time in the centuries still far ahead may serve a useful purpose. It can help to put our present troubles in their true perspective—and it can remind us all what we stand to lose, if we do not solve them.

ACKNOWLEDGMENTS

Grateful acknowledgment is made to the following for permission to reprint selections included in this anthology:

Corinth Books, Inc. for a selection from *A Journal of the Pilgrims at Plymouth (Mourt's Relation)*, edited and with an introduction by Dwight B. Heath, New York, 1963.

The Bobbs-Merrill Company, Inc. for a selection from *A History of Travel in America* by Seymour Dunbar, copyright 1915 by the Bobbs-Merrill Company, Inc.

Robert West Howard for a selection from *The Horse in America*, 1965.

Dodd, Mead & Company, Inc. for a selection from *The Autobiography and Other Writings of Benjamin Franklin*, 1963.

Yale University Press, Inc. for a selection from *The Travels of William Bartram*, edited by Francis Harper, copyright 1958 by Yale University Press, Inc.

Houghton Mifflin Company and The Mount Vernon Ladies Association of the Union for selections from *The Diaries of George Washington 1748-1799, Volume 4*, edited by John C. Fitzpatrick, copyright 1925 by The Mount Vernon Ladies Association of the Union.

Houghton Mifflin Company for a selection from *The Journals of Lewis and Clark*, edited by Bernard DeVoto, copyright 1953 by Houghton Mifflin Company.

Horizon Press for a selection from *The Dictionary of Humorous Quotations*, edited by Evan Esar, published by Horizon Press, copyright 1949 by Evan Esar.

Citadel Press, Inc. for a selection from *A History of Roads* by Geoffrey Hindley, published by Citadel Press (a division of Lyle Stuart, Inc.), Secaucus, New Jersey 1971.

Johnson Reprint Corporation for a selection from *The United States and Canada, 1832, 1833, 1834* by Carl David Arfwedson, 1834, reprinted in 1969.

Macmillan Publishing Co., Inc. for a selection from *Folk Laughter on the American Frontier* by Mody C. Boatright, New York, 1949. Copyright 1942, 1943, 1945, 1949 by Mody C. Boatright, renewed 1970, 1971, 1973 by Elizabeth K. Boatright, Frances B. Speck and Mody K. Boatright.

Macmillan Publishing Co., Inc. for a selection from *A Hawaiian Anthology*, edited by Gerrit Judd, 1967.

Jo Stewart, International Creative Management for selections from *Diary of America*, edited by Josef and Dorothy Berger, published by Simon and Schuster, 1957. Reprinted by permission of Jo Stewart, ICM, copyright 1957 by Josef and Dorothy Berger.

Corner House Publishers for selections from *The Prairie Traveler* by Randolph B. Marcy, Harper & Bros., New York, 1859, reprinted 1968 by Corner House Publishers, Williamstown, Mass.

Harcourt Brace Jovanovich, Inc. for a selection from *Abraham Lincoln: The Prairie Years and the War Years*, copyright 1954 by Carl Sandburg. Reprinted by permission of Harcourt Brace Jovanovich, Inc.

The Saturday Evening Post and Will Rogers, Jr. for an excerpt from *The Autobiography of Will Rogers*. Reprinted by permission from The Saturday Evening Post, copyright 1926, 1927, 1928, 1929, 1932 by The Curtis Publishing Company.

Alfred A. Knopf, Inc. for a selection from *North America* by Anthony Trollope, edited by Donald Smalley and Bradford A. Booth, 1951.

Little, Brown and Company for "The Railway Train," from *The Complete Poems of Emily Dickinson*.

Harper & Row, Publishers, Inc. for abridgement of chapters II, III, IV of *Roughing It* by Mark Twain (Harper and Row). Reprinted by permission of the publishers.

Funk & Wagnalls, Inc. for a selection from *Our Vanishing Landscape* by Eric Sloane, copyright 1955 by Wilfred Funk, Inc.

Xerox University Microfilms for a selection from *Travel and Adventure in the Territory of Alaska* by Frederick Whymper.

Yankee, Inc. for "The Most Sensational Walk in American History," by Irwin Ross. Reprinted with permission from *The 1974 Old Farmer's Almanac*, published in Dublin, N.H., copyright 1973.

University of Oklahoma Press for a selection from *A Lady's Life in the Rocky Mountains* by Isabella L. Bird. New edition copyright 1960 by the University of Oklahoma Press.

Little, Brown and Company for a selection from *The Mustangs* by J. Frank Dobie, copyright 1952 by J. Frank Dobie.

Houghton Mifflin Company for a selection from *The Wilderness World of John Muir*, edited by Edwin Way Teale, copyright 1954 by Edwin Way Teale.

Margaret K. O'Malley and M. Alicia O'Malley for "Moving Day For the Second" (our title) by D.J. O'Malley. This article first appeared in *The Rocky Mountain Husbandman*, Great Falls, Montana, July 2, 1936.

University of Oklahoma Press for a selection from *Up the Trail in '79* by Baylis John Fletcher. New edition copyright 1968 by the University of Oklahoma Press.

Charles Scribner's Sons for "Theodore Roosevelt in Cowboy Land" (our title). Reprinted by permission of Charles Scribner's Sons from *The Autobiography of Theodore Roosevelt*, edited by Wayne Andrews. Copyright 1913 Charles Scribner's Sons.

Southwest Heritage Magazine for "Last Day With the Dogies" by J.M. Hanson.

Scripps-Howard Newspapers for a selection from *Home Country* by Ernie Pyle, copyright by Scripps-Howard Newspaper Alliance.

Dodd, Mead & Company for "Riding to Town," from *The Complete Poems of Paul Laurence Dunbar*.

Doubleday & Co., Inc. for "On 'The Open Road,' " from *Midstream*, copyright 1929 by Helen Keller and The Crowell Publishing Company. Reprinted by permission of Doubleday & Co., Inc.

McGraw-Hill Book Company for selections from *A Long Way From Boston* by Beth O'Shea, copyright 1946 by Beth O'Shea. Used by permission of McGraw-Hill Book Company.

Funk & Wagnalls, Inc. for a selection from *Return to Taos* by Eric Sloane, copyright 1960 by Wilfred Funk, Inc.

Charles Scribner's Sons for "Toonerville Trolley." Reprinted by permission from *Toonerville Trolley*, published by Charles Scribner's Sons.

Charles Scribner's Sons for "Roosevelt Field, May 20, 1927" (our title). Reprinted by permission of Charles Scribner's Sons from *The Spirit of St. Louis* by Charles A. Lindbergh. Copyright 1953 Charles Scribner's Sons.

Saturday Review for a selection from "The Bowling Green" by Christopher Morley. Copyright 1936 by Saturday Review.

Harper & Row, Publishers, Inc. for "Ask That Man" by Robert Benchley, from *The Benchley Roundup*, edited by Nathaniel Benchley, copyright 1925 by Harper & Row, Publishers, Inc. Reprinted by permission of the publishers.

Robert C. Dille for a selection from *Collected Works of Buck Rogers*, edited by Robert C. Dille, copyright 1929-1969 National Newspaper Syndicate, Inc.

Simon and Schuster, Inc. for a selection from *We Seven* by The Astronauts Themselves, copyright 1962 by Simon and Schuster, Inc., reprinted by permission of the publisher.

The New York Times Company for a selection from *We Reach the Moon* by John Noble Wilford, W. W. Norton & Co., New York, copyright 1971 by The New York Times Company. Reprinted by permission.

Little, Brown and Company for a selection from *First on the Moon, A Voyage With Neil Armstrong, Michael Collins, Edwin A. Aldrin, Jr.*, written with Gene Farmer and Dora Jane Hamblin, epilogue by Arthur C. Clarke, copyright 1970 by Little, Brown and Company.

E. P. Dutton & Co., Inc. for "The Plains Were Black With Buffalo" (our title), from *West of the West* by Robert Kirsch and William S. Murphy. Copyright 1967 by Robert Kirsch and William S. Murphy. Reprinted by permission of the publishers, E. P. Dutton & Co., Inc.

In addition, special thanks to The Joint Free Public Library of Morristown and Morris Township, Morristown, New Jersey.